Wild
Animals
of North America

Whales Great & Small

Order Cetacea

Awful jawful of stiletto teeth arms the killer whale for hunting. In common with other cetaceans— whose land ancestors adapted to life in the sea—killer whales must surface to breathe.

"There is no proper place for them in a *scala naturae*," wrote zoologist George Gaylord Simpson in 1945 as he struggled to classify the cetaceans. "They may be imagined as extending into a different dimension from any of the surrounding orders. . . ."

Although classified by the ancients as fish, the cetaceans are mammals. They feed their young with mother's milk and they possess, at least in fetal life, traces of a hairy coat.

The cetaceans of the world include 77 species, of which 47 swim in North American waters and tropical portions of the North Pacific Ocean, including waters off Hawaii. About half of the species are known as whales, the others as dolphins or porpoises. It's not important whether one calls a small cetacean a dolphin or a porpoise, although some people distinguish "dolphin" as a cetacean having a distinct snout or beak, while "porpoise" usually means one having a smoothly rounded forehead. The variety of common names applied to cetaceans reflects the bewilderment of early seafarers as they tried to classify these unlikely beasts.

Commercial whale hunters use the name "great whales" for the ten largest and most valuable species, including (in order of bulk) the blue, right, bowhead, fin, sperm, humpback, gray, sei, Bryde's, and minke.

Modern cetaceans, wholly aquatic, probably evolved from land mammals 60 million years ago during Paleocene time. On the evidence of blood chemistry—which represents a sort of genetic-memory storage bank—the land ancestors of the cetaceans were similar to the ancestors of today's cattle and sheep. Presumably those pioneer predecessors emigrated from the continents, and groups of their descendants evolved into the mysticetes (the baleen cetaceans) and the odontocetes (the toothed cetaceans). Cetaceans

must have been preceded by forms that lived along seacoasts and in brackish waters, but no fossils of such forms have been found.

Although the slender, snakelike archaeocetes, the oldest fossil forms, date back 45 million years, their bone structure tells us that they were unmistakably whales. All are now extinct. Nearly as ancient are the oldest odontocetes, some of which later may have given rise to the mysticetes.

All cetaceans "remember" their geologic past in anatomical traces known as vestiges or relics. All retain a few coarse hairs up to the time of birth, while some keep several hundred throughout life. Adults have vestigial hips or slender bones embedded in the flank muscles. Fetal whales have hind-leg buds that disappear before birth, and one in many thousands is born with tiny, partly formed hind legs protruding from its body.

The ancestors of whales entered the shallows of the Paleocene ocean hunting for fish and shellfish. As they ventured farther and farther to sea, they were challenged by a new and unfriendly environment which was chilling, fluid, and three-dimensional. (It was also salty, but that seems not to have bothered them.) How did they adapt? All cetacean peculiarities of form and function are easily understandable if one reflects on these three challenges of sea life.

In the chill waters of the ocean, a large volume-to-surface ratio is an advantage to an animal in maintaining a sufficient body temperature. Through natural selection, whales became large-bodied. The smallest cetacean in North American waters (a newborn harbor porpoise) weighs 12 to 16 pounds; the largest (an adult female blue whale) up to 200 tons. Even tropical cetaceans are large, for the thermal conductivity of water is more than 20 times that of air, which means that a warm-blooded animal immersed in cooler water tends to lose heat rapidly.

All cetacean species normally give birth to a single well-developed baby, called a calf, fully able to withstand the chill of the sea.

And all cetaceans are enveloped in warm blubber—a tissue rich in fat which lies just beneath the skin. In a large whale, the blubber may be two feet thick and represent 45 percent of the body weight. It serves not only as insulation but as a food depot to be tapped for energy during the long fasts which many of the cetaceans typically undergo, especially during the mating season.

Influenced by fluid pressures in this new environment, through natural selection the typical cetacean body has become fusiform, torpedo-shaped. The hind legs have disappeared; the forelimbs have become flippers with their joints rigidly locked from the shoulder outward; genital organs and nipples have sunk into pockets where they rest when

not in service; and the external ears have become tiny pits in the skin. The ear opening of a full-grown blue whale is about the diameter of a pencil lead. Nostrils—one in odontocetes, two in mysticetes—are now on top of the head, where they enable the cetacean to "blow" or quickly exchange its breath. The nasal passages do not open into the throat as in land mammals but smoothly join the windpipe. Thus, when a cetacean swims with its mouth open, water does not enter its lungs.

At the tip of the tail are the flukes—wide, horizontally flattened vanes of muscle, tendon, and gristle stiffened axially by the tip of the backbone. Powerful up-and-down movements of the afterbody and the flukes furnish the main thrust in swimming. According to one zoologist's calculations, an 85-foot blue whale swimming at a top speed of 20 knots uses 276 horsepower.

"I once watched an eight-foot bottlenosed porpoise being netted off Cape Hatteras," wrote zoologist Remington Kellogg, "and was astonished by the strength in his tail. A foolhardy onlooker tried to stand on the flukes. With an effortless flip, the porpoise tossed him several feet."

I myself have often looked down on dolphins racing beside the bow of a ship and marveled at their easy, careless motion. They glide as though pulled by invisible wires.

The killer whale, largest of the dolphin family, may be the speediest of all cetaceans; it can sprint at 26 knots.

Whalemen have coined names for characteristic postures and movements of whales. In *sounding,* the whale lifts its tail flukes high in the air and dives almost vertically. In *breaching,* it jumps clear of the water and falls on its side or belly with a great splash. In *lobtailing,* it stands vertically with its head underwater while thrashing the surface into foam with its tail. In *spy-hopping,* it assumes a posture like a floating bottle, lifting its head into the air and searching the horizon.

While most land mammals live in horizontal space, cetaceans live also in vertical space. They move up and down in the sea, locating

food, dodging enemies, and keeping contact with one another. They have acquired organs and skills that enable them to read the vibrations, both sounds and ultrasounds, always flooding them in their boundless environment. In turn, cetaceans give off signals of various kinds, some poetically called voices or songs. By emitting signals some whales not only talk to one another but recognize through echolocation the kinds of fishes they are pursuing, the shape of the sea floor, and

the shape and texture of other submarine objects. The ability to echolocate has not been shown in baleen whales, perhaps because typically they passively "graze" plankton and don't chase individual fishes and squids.

Cetaceans can vocalize at rates as low as 20 cycles per second, making a sound like the creak of a rusty hinge, or as high as 256,000 cycles. The human ear can pick up sounds no shriller than 20,000 cycles. At full volume, a whale's underwater sounds may carry for hundreds—perhaps thousands—of miles. X-ray studies have shown that in the bottlenose dolphin some sounds are produced within a complex system of nasal sacs rather than within the throat.

Most cetaceans see fairly well both in and

Straining for a living, a baleen whale (opposite) opens cavernous jaws to gulp seawater rich in plankton. Baleen plates sieve the sea soup, retaining shrimplike krill, staple food of these whales.

A movable feast, shoals of krill swarm in the oceans—perhaps 500 million to 5 billion tons of animal protein. A humpback may use its tongue to roll krillballs, downing 1,300 pounds at one meal.

out of water, although their eyes are short-sighted (myopic) in air. Judging from their brain anatomy, they have little or no sense of smell. Their sense of taste has been little studied. Odontocetes lack typical mammalian taste buds, but they do show preference in an aquarium for one kind of chopped fish over another.

Their diving and breath-holding abilities continue to astound us. The body of an unfortunate sperm whale was found tangled in a

for two hours before it emerged to breathe.

In the vast, fluid, and trackless medium in which cetaceans live, many species have found advantage, or survival value, in perfecting the behavior trait known as mutual aid. They will instantly help a companion in distress, offering support with their flippers or body, or standing by in what appears to be sympathy. Care-giving behavior resembles human kindness and is one reason why people like cetaceans.

Earning a name and a livelihood, killer whales attack a 60-foot blue whale, the world's largest animal species. Hunting communally, a pod of about 30 orcas penned the blue, then moved in, ripping its flesh.

cable 3,720 feet below the surface. Sperm whales are believed (on the evidence of radio-tracking and sonar) to descend to 10,000 feet or more.

Gunners of a Norwegian whaling station told physiologist P. F. Scholander that a sperm whale can remain below the surface "spontaneously" for at least one hour, while a bottlenose (*Hyperoodon*) can beat its performance. He was told of a harpooned bottlenose that had remained underwater

Off Vancouver Island, British Columbia, a ferry captain saw a vivid demonstration of care-giving by the killer whale, "wolf of the sea" that chases and eats other warm-blooded mammals. Hearing a crunch astern, the captain turned the ferry about. To his dismay he saw a young killer whale, one of a family of four, wallowing in the sea. "The cow and the bull," he said, "cradled the injured calf between them to prevent it from turning upside down. Occasionally the bull would lose its position and the calf would roll over on its side. When this occurred, the slashes caused by our propellor were quite visible."

Another reason for the popular interest in cetaceans is the widely held notion that these animals are intelligent. Are cetaceans as intelligent as our own species? True, the sperm whale has the largest brain (up to 20.2 pounds) of any animal on earth. In the laboratory, a dolphin has been trained to crudely imitate the speech of its trainer. Consider, if

Or compare the ratio of "new brain" (neo-cortical) tissue to whole brain tissue. It is low in primitive mammals and high in recently evolved ones. Percentages of new brain tissue are, for the common dolphin 97.8, man 95.9, dog 84.2, rabbit 56.0, and hedgehog 32.4. Score again for the dolphin!

However, the original question *should not have been asked*. The big, convoluted brains of the dolphin and the human evolved in distinctly separate worlds. The one organ now

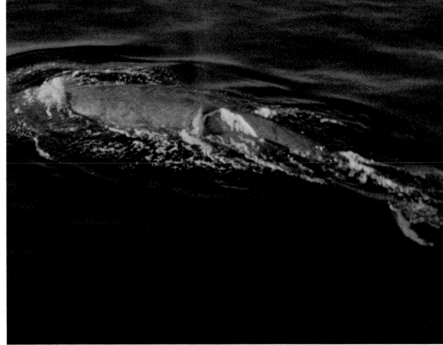

you will, comparative brain weights. Remove the blubber coat that makes up about 40 percent of a bottlenose dolphin's weight; the brain then represents 2.0 percent of its body. The brain of a naked man represents only 1.7 percent. Score for the dolphin!

Then look at the ratio, brain weight to spinal cord weight in the two mammals. (In general, the higher the ratio the greater the intelligence). It is about 40 to 1 in the dolphin and 50 to 1 in humans. Score for us!

represents a climax of "whaleness," the other of "primateness." Instead of wondering whether dolphins can reason, or worry, or plan ahead as we humans can, we should be content to admire them for their unique minds and bodies—for their vital architecture that allows them to live in a forbidding world of water where our own naked selves could not long survive.

What little is known of the mating of great whales has been learned through tantalizing

Hours later, the assault halts— reason unknown—and the pack leaves the prey. Minus dorsal fin and bleeding from a 6-foot-square wound in its side, the blue swims feebly, perhaps soon to die.

glimpses, often from afar. During courtship, the whales may leap from the water and fall back with a resounding smash. They may give love pats with the flippers, or teasing strokes with the body surfaces, or gentle nips with the teeth. Mating may take place either as the two swim horizontally near the surface or as they rise vertically from the water in a clumsy embrace, their snouts in the air.

Mating among dolphins, however, has been recorded in great detail by trained observers peering through the windows of oceanariums. As among whales, copulation is brief, lasting only seconds, and is usually repeated. In its quick timing it resembles copulation in cattle and sheep, those ungulates thought to share ancestry with whales.

The gestation period varies with the species. Among mysticetes it ranges from $9\frac{1}{2}$ to 13 months; among odontocetes from 11 to 17 months. The mysticete fetus begins to spurt in growth as it nears full term; the odontocete fetus grows at a steadier rate.

Twin fetuses occur in about eight of every 1,000 baleen whales. It is unlikely, however, that a whale could successfully nurse two calves to the stage of independence.

One of the first play-by-play accounts of a cetacean birth was written in 1947 by Arthur F. McBride. Standing at a poolside of Marine Studios, in Florida, he had been watching a female bottlenose dolphin, its abdomen greatly swollen, which had withdrawn from her companions. I reconstruct his story:

Time Zero. Her contractions begin; she gives queer barking sounds underwater.

Minute 7. The soft, folded tail flukes of the fetus emerge and slowly relax in the water.

Minute 17. She arches her back violently, tail upward, and expels the 25-pound fetus as far as its flippers.

Minute 23. Out comes the head! The calf falls free; the mother whirls about, breaking the umbilical cord near the calf's body. The placenta is not expelled for several hours.

Minute 24. The calf instinctively swims to the surface and takes its first breath. Pool companions, intensely curious, join the pair.

Parturition in dolphins lasts from 21 minutes to several hours. Normal births are rapid, the calf usually arriving tail-first. The mother squirts milk into the funnel formed by the nursing calf's muscular little tongue.

The mysticetes are thought to nurse their young for about 6 to 11 months, the odontocetes for 18 to 25 months. The largest odontocete—the huge sperm whale—evidently nurses for two years. Dutch zoologist E. J. Slijper wrote that cetacean milk tastes like "a mixture of fish, liver, Milk of Magnesia, and oil." It has the thick texture of canned milk, and its fat content—40 to 50 percent—makes it ten times as rich as cow's milk.

Shortages of available food or seasonal periods of fasting continually interrupt cetacean growth. As a result, growth marks like the annual rings of trees are left in the teeth of odontocetes and in the baleen and waxy ear plugs of mysticetes.

Some of the longevity records among cetaceans are: white whale, 30 years; bottlenose dolphin, at least 32; northern bottlenose whale, at least 37; sperm whale 77; and fin whale, at least 80.

Navigators supreme, all the great whales migrate from cool waters where they feed in summer to warmer breeding waters in winter. How they navigate is unknown, although, like migrating birds, they doubtless use all their body senses. Their seamarks are thought to be wind currents, water currents, a myriad of underwater sounds, contours of the sea floor, water temperatures, and the position of the sun and moon.

The migration of the gray whale of the North Pacific is famous. A typical pregnant female leaves the food-rich waters of the Arctic Ocean in September and swims southward through Bering Strait to the west coast of North America. In late December she passes near San Diego, where each winter nearly a million tourists visit headlands or embark in small "wildlife safari" boats to watch the whales go by. In early January, she gives birth—along with 1,200 other mature females—in certain sheltered lagoons of

western Mexico. In March, the mother and calf turn northwestward on a course still imprecisely known to us. She weans the calf at sea in late July after nursing it for seven months. From early summer to early fall she feeds in the Bering and Chukchi seas and the Arctic Ocean. Her 10,000-mile migratory journey has come full circle.

The movements of odontocetes smaller than the sperm whale are poorly known, although it is clear that most dolphins and porpoises move seasonally (and some even daily) in response to changes in the food supply. In summer, pilot whales off the coast of Newfoundland move inshore in synchrony with the migrations of a certain squid (*Illex*) upon which they feed heavily at that season. The

white whales of polar seas are less specialized feeders. Their movements are dictated mainly by the shifting limits of the pack ice.

While the baleen whales are "grazers," the white whales, like other toothed species, are hunters. They feed on small schooling fishes, squids, and swimming crabs. (The killer whale, an exception, also preys on warm-blooded animals.) Worldwide, the odontocetes number 67 species, of which 11 are dealt with in this book. Some of these travel hundreds of miles up rivers while others (though not North American species) live landlocked in freshwater systems.

The teeth of odontocetes are typically conical, sharp, and uniform (not distinguished as incisors, canines, and molars). They vary in

Easy riders, acorn barnacles do not harm their host, a humpback, but the burden of freeloaders may build to 1,000 pounds. When a migrating whale reaches warmer seas, barnacles may drop off.

number from only two in the narwhal and in certain beaked whales to 242 in the franciscana, or La Plata dolphin. Odontocetes have permanent teeth only. Although milk teeth begin to form in fetal life, they soon disappear in the growing tissue of the gums.

The power of echolocation, well developed in odontocetes, probably less so in mysticetes, may relate to the difference in food-gathering habits. A sense of surroundings is clearly more useful to a hunter than to a grazer. The longer nursing period in toothed cetaceans also relates to food-gathering. Evidently the calf needs more time with its mother to learn complex navigational skills.

The odontocete skull is asymmetrical and is telescoped, as if pushed from the front. The two nostrils unite before they reach the surface, then open in a single crescentic blowhole. Within the head, the nostrils flare into oddly shaped chambers or vestibular sacs. These probably function in sound production. They are absent in mysticetes.

Most odontocetes are smaller than mysticetes. The smallest in North America, the harbor porpoise, weighs, as an average adult, 100 to 130 pounds. Odontocete males are nearly always larger than females.

The mysticetes, toothless whales, number ten species worldwide, nine in North American waters. These cetaceans gather food by means of peculiar outgrowths of the upper gums known as baleen (a word both singular and plural). Early American whalers spoke of baleen as "whalebone," although it is not bone. It is a black, white, yellowish, or gray substance textured like fingernail, densely fringed with hairlike bristles on its inner, or tongue, side. The name mysticetes incorporates a Greek word for mustache.

Baleen is a series of plates arranged like the shutters of an open Venetian blind. The plates reach their climax development in the bowhead whale, where they may number 360 on each side of the jaw. Some of the plates are fourteen feet long.

Plankton organisms known as krill are trapped by the baleen plates and are probably rolled into balls by the tongue and currents of water. They then pass into the slender throat and are rhythmically swallowed. Commercial fishermen along the Nova Scotia coast keep a sharp lookout for baleen whales, for both whales and fish (especially herring) are likely to gather where krill is abundant. Thus whales are indicators of fish schools. An astounding biomass of krill, estimated as high as five billion tons, is the greatest potential source of animal protein in the world. (Whales found this out long before we did.)

Baleen whales also differ from toothed species in being exclusively oceanic. They also are large (5 to 200 tons), the females being slightly larger than the males. They have paired blowholes, and they have symmetrical skulls in which the bones are telescoped, as though shoved from behind. They are "hairier" than odontocetes, having numerous coarse "whiskers" (vibrissae) around the jaws and on top of the head.

Ocean life, like life on land, presents a variety of hazards. Cetaceans suffer many of the same ailments which distress people. They are attacked by bacterial, fungal, and viral diseases, including pneumonia and tuberculosis; they suffer cancers and stomach ulcers; their bodies harbor parasitic worms. Certain other "fellow travelers" which attach to their skin, teeth, or baleen do no harm. These include diatoms, other algae, protozoans, barnacles, tiny crustaceans called "whale lice," and suckerfish or remoras.

We continually dump contaminants into the sea, threatening marine life. Poisons such as insecticides, weed killers, lead from automobile exhausts, and manufacturing wastes such as cadmium, mercury, and arsenic find their way into the sea. Here they enter the bodies of primary producers, mainly diatoms. Many poisons resist natural decay, so they end up in the bodies of cetaceans—the organisms highest on the food ladder.

Collectors for a Florida aquarium saved a rare, 570-pound pygmy sperm whale found on a beach. The whale died a week later; it had swallowed a large plastic bag of the kind fishermen carry on their boats. Cetaceans make headline news when they run aground in pods numbering 200 or more. The stranded species are nearly always odontocetes. Because echolocation is known to be highly developed in odontocetes but not in mysticetes, some scientists believe that failure of the echolocation system may cause strandings. If a pilot whale, for instance, overshoots its prey and finds itself helpless in shallow water, its frantic calls of distress may draw its

erant—up to a point—of the other's presence. Porpoise remains have been found in shark stomachs and vice versa. In one find, a little harbor porpoise had choked to death while trying to swallow a four-foot shark.

Man, of course, is the archenemy of cetacean life. Abusive commercial whaling, stimulated by development of the explosive harpoon in the 1860's and the self-contained factory ship in the early 1900's, may have doomed several species to extinction. The

companions. Soon the shallows are filled with confusing "white noise" signals and exhausted animals. One cause of echolocation failure and stranding is thought to be parasitic worms that invade the brain by way of the nasal sinuses and ear openings.

The theory has been advanced that cetaceans turn to the land in times of distress because they "remember" the safety it provided for their terrestrial ancestors tens of millions of years ago. Although the theory has a certain romantic appeal, it seems unlikely.

The cetaceans have few enemies. Killer whales are known to attack and eat other cetaceans, while sharks prey on dolphins. As a rule, however, sharks and cetaceans seem to maintain a sort of watchful truce. Each is tol-

reported kill (which is less than the total kill) of great whales in the peak decade of whaling, 1956-1965, was more than 600,000.

By the end of the 1970's, the great whales in the Northern Hemisphere were down to about 44 percent of their prewhaling numbers and to 33 percent of their prewhaling biomass. (Corresponding figures for the Southern Hemisphere—the region exploited most intensively—are 24 and 18 percent).

The blue whale, humpback, and bowhead may be below 10 percent of their original numbers, perhaps never to recover. So complex are the unknowns and the unknowables in marine ecosystems that zoologists can't predict the future of whale populations reduced to such levels.   VICTOR B. SCHEFFER

Born eyes open and able to swim, a pilot whale calf gets a jet assist at suckling time. Mother squirts her milk speedily so the calf can surface. Some newborn whales breathe every 30 seconds or so.

OVERLEAF: *Headed for the deep, says the tail of a humpback. One of the imperiled giants, the humpback is acclaimed for its vocalizations. In concert season—winter—song resounds through its watery realm.*

Family Eschrichtiidae

This family consists of a single species, the gray whale of the North Pacific Ocean. Formerly, perhaps as recently as the 18th century, it lived also in the North Atlantic. Gray whale bones of somewhat less than fossil age have been discovered in sediments along the northwestern coast of Europe in England, Sweden, and the Netherlands.

The map shows the gray whale's migration route and the location of major summer populations.

Gray Whale (*Eschrichtius robustus*)

To North Americans, the gray whale is the best known of all the cetaceans, for millions of people have seen it passing southward near the southern California coast in midwinter. People have also observed it in the lagoons of Baja California in Mexico where it breeds after its 5,000-mile migration from polar seas. Reduced by hunting in the early 1900's, it was given protection in 1937. Its numbers have now leveled off between 11,000 and 15,000.

In February 1972, the Mexican Government established a new national whale refuge—the world's first—to protect the gray whale nursery in Scammon Lagoon.

The gray whale has been called a "living fossil." Its skull, in particular, is constructed along the general lines of whales that lived millions of years ago.

It differs from other baleen whales in that it often feeds inshore among rocks and kelp; it may even play in the surf.

The gray whale is found in shallow waters on both sides of the North Pacific from the Arctic

Ocean to Mexico. Commercial hunting had drastically reduced the western Pacific, or Korean, stock by the early 1930's. Very few individuals of the original Asian stock are known to survive.

In the eastern Pacific stock, a typical pregnant female leaves Alaskan waters in September. She swims southward at 5 miles an hour, travels some 100 miles a day, and arrives in Scammon Lagoon in December. There she gives birth. (She will not remate for a year or two.) She and the calf leave the lagoon in early March and swim slowly northward. About

the end of July she weans the seven-month-old calf.

Gray whales migrate singly or in groups of as many as 16. Not all individuals follow the established migration pattern. They may be seen throughout the year in the Gulf of California, off the Farallon Islands west of San Francisco, and off Vancouver Island, British Columbia, and at other points along the coast.

The gray whale evidently does not feed during its southward migration but lives on fat. It loses

about one-fifth of its weight while in winter quarters south of San Francisco. In summer it feeds largely on amphipods near the floor of the ocean.

Male and female grays mature sexually between ages 5 and 11. They mate in late November and early December; the gestation period is 13 months. They reach full size at age 40 and are known to live to at least 69.

Gigi, a two-ton, 19-foot yearling gray whale, was captured in Scammon Lagoon in 1971 and successfully held in a San Diego oceanarium for a year.

When she became too costly to feed, she was released in the open sea with a radio transmitter pinned to her dorsal ridge. Navy scientists tracked her position along the coast of southern California for seven weeks, until her signals faded into silence.

The record length for a female is 49 feet (15 m) and weight 35.2 tons (32 t); for a male, 47 feet (14 m) and 27 tons (24.5 t). The newborn calf measures about 16 feet (5 m) long and weighs about 900 pounds (408 kg).

Family Balaenopteridae

These furrow-throated whales are called "rorquals," a name derived from an old Norwegian word. Skin furrows running from the point of the chin to the chest expand like accordion pleats when a rorqual opens its jaws in a wide "yawn," increasing its water intake. The rorquals are also called "fin whales." The term, however, is not distinctive, for many species outside this family also have a dorsal fin.

Besides having furrows, the rorquals are distinguished from the right whale by a wider skull, coarser and less flexible baleen, unfused neck vertebrae, and longer, more tapering flippers. The rorquals have lost one finger bone in each flipper, while all other cetacean species retain the primitive five.

Within this family are six of the world's great whales: the blue, fin, sei, Bryde's, minke, and humpback. All six can be seen in North American waters.

Fin Whale (*Balaenoptera physalus*)

During the 19th century, the fin whale, with a population of about 450,000, was the most common baleen whale. In spite of hunting pressure it is still one of the most common.

The fin whale has been called "greyhound of the sea," for powerful muscles can push its tapering body to speeds up to 20 knots through the sea and to submarine depths of at least 755 feet. Unlike the blue and sei whales, the fin whale sometimes will leap clear of the water, falling back with a tremendous splash.

For some unknown reason, the right side of the head is paler in color than the left.

The finback may measure to 76.1 feet (23 m) and weigh 70.8 tons (64.2 t). Size of the newborn calf is about 21 feet (6 m) and 2.09 tons (1.9 t). Roy Chapman Andrews wrote that an Alaskan 65-foot fin whale discharged a 22-foot fetus as her body was being drawn up the slip of a whaling station.

Fin whales range through all oceans, but are rare in tropical waters or amid pack ice. They sometimes are found singly or in pairs but more often occur in pods of six or seven. Many pods with as many as 50 animals may concentrate in a small area. A pelagic species, it is not often seen near shore.

Many individual finbacks do not migrate in fall to warmer waters but remain in subpolar waters where food is more abundant.

The diet is mainly krill but includes anchovies, capelin, herring, lantern fish, and other small fishes, as well as squid.

Blue Whale (*Balaenoptera musculus*)

The largest animal that has ever lived, this bluish-gray whale was feared by open-boat whalers of the 19th century because of its powerful flukes and its speed when wounded—up to 20 knots. By the early 1900's, whalers began hunting the animals in fast, steam-powered catcher boats, killing them with fragmentation bombs fired from cannon, and butchering them at sea aboard huge floating factories. In 1931, the whalers of the world killed 29,606 blue whales. Blue whales have been protected since 1966 by all those nations adhering to the International Whaling Convention. Some zoologists doubt that the blue whale will ever recover from over-hunting. In the late 1970's, the North Pacific population was still only 1,500 or so; the North Atlantic perhaps a few hundred.

The largest blue whale both measured and weighed (piecemeal) was a female brought to the whaling station at South Georgia in the southern Atlantic about 1931. She was 96.8 feet (30 m) long and weighed about 196 tons (177.8 t). Whales slightly longer than 100 feet (30 m) have been reported. A 100-foot female at the peak of her feeding season in

the Antarctic summer might weigh as much as 215 tons (195 t).

Blue whales of North American waters feed in summer in the Gulf of Alaska, along the Aleutian Islands (rarely in the Bering Sea), and in Davis Strait. In winter, they breed off western Mexico and at an unknown place somewhere in warm waters of the North Atlantic or Caribbean Sea. Blue whales usually travel singly or in pairs.

Blues feed almost entirely on shrimplike krill and may eat over a ton at one feeding. Canadian zoologist David E. Sergeant estimates the daily food demand of a baleen whale is two to four percent of its body weight. Thus, a 200-ton blue whale may consume four to eight tons of krill a day.

Male and female mature sexually at about ten years of age. Every two or three years, during winter, the female gives birth after a 12-month gestation period. When the calf is weaned at about seven months, it has gained an average of seven to eight pounds an hour throughout its entire suckling period.

Many tales are told of the blue whale's strength and stamina. One harpooned individual towed the steam-whaler *Puma*, with her engines running at half-speed astern, for nearly 24 hours.

Sei Whale (*Balaenoptera borealis*)

Norwegian fishermen gave this whale its name because it arrives on their coasts at the same time as the *sei* or pollock. Smaller and less valuable than its cousins the blue, fin, and humpback, the sei whale was largely ignored by whale hunters until they had depleted the larger species. Along the Pacific Coast, the sei ranges from the Aleutian Islands in summer to Mexico in winter, and along the Atlantic Coast from Davis Strait in summer to the Caribbean in winter. They travel in small groups of two to five but form larger aggregations while at the feeding grounds.

In the far north the sei whale feeds on copepods and other plankton organisms. In the lower latitudes the diet includes small schooling fishes—sauries, anchovies, herring, sardines, jack mackerel— as well as krill. The uncommonly fine, soft-textured fibers that fringe the baleen are an advantage in capturing organisms as small as copepods. A 47-foot sei whale was examined by scientists of Japan's Whales Research Institute. The plankton-straining surface of the whale's baleen amounted to 39 square feet. Thus, every time a sei whale squishes a mouthful of seawater through its baleen it is,

Bryde's Whale (*Balaenoptera edeni*)

Bryde's whale, whose common name honors the captain of a Norwegian whaling vessel, is similar to the sei in appearance but smaller. It lives in the tropical and warm temperate regions of the Atlantic, Pacific, and Indian oceans.

Until the middle of the 1900's whalers confused it with the sei. On close inspection, Bryde's can be distinguished by three lengthwise ridges on its snout as compared to the sei whale's one. Its baleen is stiffer and not as fine as that of the sei, and it captures coarser food. Schooling fishes—herring, mackerel, anchovies, and others—are important foods. A Bryde's once swallowed a two-foot shark.

Making deeper dives than the shallow-feeding sei, Bryde's also has a higher "blow" as it surfaces. It rises steeply, showing much of the head, rolls its body, and humps its tail without raising the flukes as it begins another dive.

The largest known Bryde's was 45.2 feet (14 m) in length and weighed 17.8 tons (16.1 t).

in effect, casting a net nearly as large as a kingsize bed. One sei whale that was measured had managed to pack 502 pounds of plankton into its stomach.

The sei has reached a length of 53.8 feet (16 m) and a normal weight of at least 23.8 tons (21.6 t). A very large, pregnant one weighed 41.6 tons (37.7 t).

Humpback Whale (*Megaptera novaeangliae*)

The chunky, slow-moving, amiable humpback is known to millions of armchair mariners who read about whales, listen to their recorded voices, or watch them on television. A humpback breaching against a deep blue sky has become a symbolic picture of all great whales.

Its long flippers, up to 14.3 feet (4 m) long, and its head adorned with fleshy knobs and white barnacles are among characteristic features.

The humpbacks of the world were wastefully hunted until 1966, when they were afforded complete protection. By then, only a few thousands were left, perhaps seven percent of their original numbers.

The largest known is 51.8 feet (16 m) and about 51 tons (46.3 t). At birth a calf measures about 15 feet (5 m) and weighs 1.4 tons (1.3 t).

The humpback ranges the eastern North Pacific Ocean from the Chukchi Sea south to southern California during the summer, and from southern California south to the Revillagigedo Islands and Jalisco, Mexico, and also around the Hawaiian Islands, during the winter. In the western North Atlantic Ocean it ranges from Disko Bay in western Greenland south to Massachusetts during the summer, and from Hispaniola and Puerto Rico south to Trinidad during the winter.

Its diet consists mainly of krill, and also small schooling fishes. One humpback killed in the North Atlantic had in its stomach six fish-eating birds (cormorants)—and a seventh stuck in its throat.

Charles Jurasz, high school science teacher and whalewatcher in southeastern Alaska, has often seen humpbacks creating a "bubble net" to capture herring and krill. "One day," he writes, "I noticed bubbles rising to the surface a short distance away. They formed a perfect circle, and just as the last few bubbles surfaced, there was a tremendous boil of fish right in the middle. Then suddenly a whale surged up from the bottom—mouth opened like a cavern—big enough to swallow me and the skiff."

Northern humpbacks mate between October and March and

Minke Whale (*Balaenoptera acutorostrata*)

calve after a gestation period of 12 to 13 months; the calf nurses for about 11 months. An adult "escort" whale often stays close to a mother-and-calf pair.

Canadian zoologist Peter Beamish once studied a female that had become entangled in a fishing net and was later removed to a holding pen. He temporarily blindfolded the docile whale and allowed her to swim through a maze of metal poles. Although she made clicking noises, these evidently did not help her to echolocate, for she repeatedly hit the poles.

Long ago, a Norwegian whaler named Meincke harpooned one of these whales, mistaking it for a blue. His companions were so amused at his error they began to speak of "Meincke's whale"— now called "minke."

This smallest of the rorquals, distinguished by a white band on each flipper, is fairly common in coastal waters. Along the Pacific Coast it is found from the Chukchi Sea south to northern Baja California during the summer and from central California south to central Mexico during the winter.

Along the Atlantic Coast its range is from Baffin Bay south to Chesapeake Bay during the summer, and from the eastern Gulf of Mexico and northeastern Florida to Puerto Rico and the Virgin Islands during winter. It is most often seen singly or in groups of two or three.

The minke whale feeds mainly on small shoal fishes and krill. In the Antarctic, it has reached a length of 36.4 feet (11 m); it weighs as much as 9.8 tons (8.9 t). North American minke whales evidently do not exceed 32.8 feet (10 m). The newborn calf is about 8.5 feet (2.6 m) long.

Minkes are more likely to be seen at close range than others of the rorqual family, for they appear to be curious about boats and may swim close to an anchored or slowly moving vessel.

In 1957 a party of British explorers traveling on the sea ice off Antarctica came upon several pools in the ice through which minke, killer, and beaked whales were rising at intervals to breathe. The whales had been trapped by the sudden freezing of a shallow harbor entrance. The men formed a Pat-the-Whale Club for those who touched a whale's snout as it rose.

Natives of the Aleutian Islands used to kill minke whales with stone-tipped harpoons dipped in the juice of a poisonous plant, monkshood (*Aconitum*). During the Middle Ages, Norwegian hunters killed minke whales with "death arrows" dipped in fluid from a rotten whale. After several days, the victim weakened and could be harpooned. Strangely, its flesh was eaten without ill effects.

Family Balaenidae

Early whale hunters named these the "right" whales because they could easily be approached in a small boat and because their harpooned bodies, rich in valuable oil, would float after death.

The arched upper jaws in right whales give the mouth its great capacity to hold water. The floor of the mouth is shaped like a gigantic scoop or spoon. (In balaenopterids, "accordion pleats" on the throat give similar capacity.) The huge skull makes up 25 to 40 percent of the length of the skeleton. Where the seven neck vertebrae join the skull, they are fused into a single bone. The right and left baleen rows do not form a continuous horseshoe shape but are separated by a gap at the snout.

Excepting the pygmy right whale of the Southern Hemisphere, the right whales have no dorsal fin.

Right Whale (*Balaena glacialis*)

What is known of the form and coloration of the now uncommon right whale, or black right whale, of North American waters is based on a few specimens killed under permit for scientific study. The body is black or slaty gray, usually with white patches of irregular shape on the underbody. On the snout in front of the blowholes the right whale bears rough, fleshy bumps which are commonly infested with "whale lice" (actually crustaceans) and barnacles; the whole region is known as the "bonnet."

The record size of a right whale is 60 feet (18 m), and its estimated weight 120 tons (108.9 t). Size of a newborn calf is believed to be less than 19.6 feet (6 m) long. A suckling calf 21.3 feet (6.5 m) long was collected in South Africa. The testes of the full-grown male right whale are enormous. One pair weighed by Japanese scientists tipped the scales at 2,143 pounds (972 kg).

The species is distributed through the temperate oceans of the world. The migratory courses in the Northern Hemisphere are poorly known, though right whales move north in summer and south in the winter.

William A. Watkins and William E. Schevill, at Woods Hole Oceanographic Institution, observed right whales near Cape Cod every year for 20 years. They concluded that the whales congregate in the spring and early summer "singly, in groups of three to eight animals, in adult pairs, and in cow

Bowhead Whale (*Balaena mysticetus*)

and calf pairs. Occasionally loose aggregations are formed with up to 30 animals within a few square kilometers."

After the whalers had nearly exterminated it, the right whale was given worldwide protection in 1935. Its numbers have grown very slowly; there are thought to be fewer than one thousand in North American waters.

Right whales feed mainly on the smaller organisms of the krill—copepods about the size of a match-head—and on young euphausids. They have been seen grazing near the surface in thickets of reddish krill, seemingly able to stay inside the richest concentrations. Watkins and Schevill once drifted within six feet of a feeding right whale. They could hear the animal's baleen plates rattling in the wind.

The bowhead was named for the resemblance of its strongly curved jaws to the shape of an archer's bow. The species has a huge and powerful head. Eskimos say that a bowhead can break its way up through ice several feet thick. The head represents more than one third the length of its body. Measuring up to 60 feet (18 m), an adult of record length would weigh about 100 tons (90.7 t). The length of a newborn calf is 13 to 15 feet (4 to 5 m).

The bowhead breeds in summer at the edge of Arctic ice, moving slowly southward in winter with the drifting floes. Its main food

source is euphausids and other crustaceans in the krill. Bowheads evidently feed sparingly during spring and fall migrations. As many as 50 may assemble in fall, but the bowhead usually travels singly or in groups of two or three. (The one above swims with belugas.)

The world population of the bowhead, including the Spitsbergen, Davis Strait, Hudson Bay, and Bering Sea stocks, was estimated in 1977 at less than 3,000. More recent estimates are slightly higher. But the population is probably less than 10 percent of its prewhaling size.

In the late 19th century the bowhead was the most valuable of all whales because it yielded

copious amounts of oil, used as fuel in household lamps, and the finest baleen, called whalebone and used mainly as corset stays.

Alaskan and Canadian Eskimos, in keeping with their cultural tradition, are still allowed to kill a few bowheads each summer; otherwise the species has been protected by all the northern nations since 1935. The Eskimos hunt from skin-covered boats called umiaks, using dart guns or shoulder guns. Either gun hurls a bomb into the whale.

Family Delphinidae

The world's delphinids, including about 40 species, are the most abundant and varied of all cetaceans. Although the larger members of this dolphin and porpoise family are called "whales," nonetheless they are typical delphinids. Unfortunately, quick identification at sea is not easy, for the main distinctive characteristics of the family are skeletal.

Delphinids have numerous conical or spatula-shaped teeth in both the upper and lower jaws, they lack throat grooves, and their tail flukes are notched. Most, though not all, have a dorsal fin.

They are mainly fish-eaters and oceanic. They feed in upper waters, surfacing to breathe several times a minute. Among bottlenose dolphins which were studied for more than a year, the average dive time per animal was 21.8 seconds.

A game fish, *Coryphaena hippurus,* is also called the dolphin, and this has caused some confusion about names. The fish and the mammals are, of course, not related. As to the difference between dolphin and porpoise, the names are often used interchangeably. But some authorities follow the sailor's choice: Any small whale species in this family is called a porpoise.

Common Dolphin (*Delphinus delphis*)

"Full of fine spirits, they invariably come from the breezy billows to windward. They are the lads that always live before the wind. They are accounted a lucky omen." Thus wrote Herman Melville of the common dolphins. They are indeed a sporting class, leaping in unison as they play at the bow of a moving vessel.

In rare instances a male may reach 8.5 feet (2.6 m) in length and weigh 300 pounds (136 kg). Females are slightly smaller. One of the most widespread and abundant dolphins in the world, it lives in warm and temperate open seas. On the coasts of

North America it ranges from Oregon to Costa Rica, and from Newfoundland to the Caribbean. Common dolphins may gather in groups of several thousand.

Two zoologists once watched common dolphins off the coast of California feeding on sardines, anchovies, sauries, small bonito, and squid. Several dolphins drove the prey clear out of the water—and caught it in midair! Their teeth are small, sharp, and recurved, perfectly adapted for catching slippery fish. A United Nations report claims that these dolphins along the California coast eat 300,000 tons of anchovies each year, whereas commercial fishermen take only 110,000 tons.

Dolphins dive deepest at night—down at least 846 feet, apparently searching for food within the "deep scattering layer" of plankton and larger organisms.

Soviet whale expert A. G. Tomilin traveled on a ship in the Black Sea carrying on deck 90 live common dolphins. All through one night he heard protests from the dolphins which reminded him "of a child's rubber toy or the short whistle of a sand grouse (lasting one or two seconds), less often, the quack of a duck or the yelp of a cat whose tail has been pinched."

Bottlenose Dolphin (*Tursiops truncatus*)

This handsome beast, familiar to millions who visit oceanariums or watch animal programs on television, is symbolic in the public mind of all dolphins. Partly from sympathy for it, the people of the United States demanded the landmark law that conserves other species as well, the Marine Mammal Protection Act of 1972.

Soon after the world's first oceanarium, Marineland, opened at St. Augustine, Florida, its manager began to wonder whether a dolphin could be taught to do tricks to entertain visitors. So in 1949 he hired Adolf Frohn, who trained wild animals for a circus, to educate Flippy, a 200-pound male bottlenose. Within several weeks, Flippy was showing his pleasure at being "in school" by leaping into Adolf's arms!

The size of the bottlenose varies considerably from place to place. The largest on record are a male 12.7 feet (3.9 m) long, from the Netherlands, and a female 10.6 feet (3.2 m) from the Bay of Biscay. A Dutch specimen 9.8 feet (3 m) long was said to weigh 882 pounds (400 kg). One report credits a weight "in excess of 1,430 pounds (649 kg)."

David and Melba Caldwell, of the University of Florida, spent many hours watching the behavior of bottlenoses at Marineland. They concluded that courtship is violent, the male and female bumping heads forcefully. Finally, "the two animals swim straight toward one another, head on, until they either hit full force . . . or glance off and slip down each other's

side. Intromission is rapid and takes place under water almost belly to belly . . ."

The newborn calf is 38.5 to 49.6 inches (98 to 126 cm) long and weighs 20 to 25 pounds (9 to 11 kg). This variation possibly includes some premature calves. Fond of warm, shallow inshore waters, the bottlenose ranges in summer as far north as Cape Hatteras, North Carolina, and in the west to Point Conception, southern California; also the year around off Hawaii. Florida has long been the center of a dolphin live-capture industry.

The bottlenose is a distinctly social species, usually traveling in groups of as many as a dozen, occasionally in aggregations of several hundred. Most populations evidently do not migrate, although they go where they can find food.

In the wild, the bottlenose feeds on squid, shrimp, and a wide variety of fishes. In some waters bottlenoses habitually follow shrimp boats, recovering what the shrimpers discard or miss. They often hunt as a team, herding small fishes, such as menhaden, ahead of them and picking off the stragglers. One day as author Scheffer was wading along a sandy Mexican beach, three bottlenoses drove a school of foot-long silvery mullet into the shallows around his feet. The dolphins wheeled to make another rush, scraping the bottom as they turned.

A blindfolded bottlenose can tell, from the nature of the echoes, the difference between a copper plate and an aluminum plate of the same size and shape.

Spinner Dolphin *(Stenella longirostris)*

This agile dolphin can leap from the sea, spin two and one-half times around the axis of its body, and plunge into the water within a second's time! Thus its name—though no one knows *why* it spins. Spinning is evidently not a courtship display, for mature and immature animals of both sexes engage in it.

Little was known of spinner dolphins until the 1960's when commercial fishermen in the tropical Pacific Ocean began to kill tens of thousands each year in newly invented nets for catching yellowfin tuna. The dolphins, trapped along with the fish in the slowly closing, or pursing, nets would suffocate.

Forced by the Marine Mammal Protection Act of 1972 to reduce the kill, fishermen improved their netting methods. Between 1971 and 1977, the kill of spinners (and associated species) dropped from 70 to 2.8 dolphins per net "set." By 1976, the population of spinner dolphins was estimated at 1,200,000, half its original level.

In the eastern tropical Pacific, the maximum known size of spinner males is 6.4 feet (2 m); of females, 6.1 feet (1.9 m).

The spinner lives in tropical inshore and offshore waters around the world, including Hawaii and the Gulf of Mexico. Little is known of its migration. In the eastern tropical Pacific its home range is roughly circular, about 200 to 300 nautical miles in diameter; it moves seasonally several hundred miles onshore (possibly in fall and winter) and offshore (possibly in spring).

The small, white earbones (otoliths) of fishes are hard, resistant to digestive juices, and characteristic for each species. Thus, an expert who examines earbones from the stomach of a sea mammal can tell what fishes were in the animal's last meal. A study of earbones from spinner dolphin stomachs disclosed that lantern fishes—tiny, pelagic, tropical fishes—composed more than half the dolphins' diet. At times spinners evidently feed more than 800 feet below the ocean surface, for the otoliths of deep-sea smelt have been found in their stomachs.

Killer Whale *(Orcinus orca)*

Unlike most cetaceans, this one preys on other warm-blooded animals. The killer whale is the marine counterpart of the tiger and wolf. A man in a boat off the California coast once saw a big male killer whale leap clear of the water, holding a full-grown sea lion crosswise in his jaws. No small feat, when a bull sea lion may weigh 600 pounds.

Another man watched a killer chasing a sea lion in the rocky shallows of the California coast. The quarry suddenly changed course, causing the killer whale to collide head on with a large rock. Stunned and quivering, it lay ten minutes before it recovered its senses and swam away.

The killer is the speedster among whales, attaining 26 knots, and is remarkably agile. Skana, a killer whale in Vancouver Public Aquarium, British Columbia, would hurl her powerful body into the air and touch a goal 23 feet above the water.

The largest male measured 32 feet long (10 m) and weighed about 9 or 10 tons (8.2 to 9.1 t); the female, 28 feet (9 m) and 5 to 6 tons (4.5 to 5.4 t).

The newborn calf is about 8 feet (2.4 m) long and weighs an estimated 400 pounds (181 kg). The Japanese have reported a 9-foot fetus and a 9-foot calf.

Worldwide in distribution, the killer whale ranges north and south to polar ice, especially near coasts. In waters of Washington and southern British Columbia, where killer whales have long been studied, the animals cruise in family units or pods of about

ten. All-white (albino) killer whales have been seen with normal ones. Their travels remind one of the seasonal, regular movements of wolf packs in the forest, except that the whales move continuously, day and night.

Japanese whaling captains who examined the stomach contents of 364 killer whales found, in order of occurrence, fishes (cod, flatfishes, sardines, salmons, tunas, and others); octopuses and squids; dolphins (Dall's, blue-white, and finless black); whales (beaked, sei, and pilot); and seals (harbor and ringed).

Dale W. Rice, whale expert for the United States Government, reported on the stomach contents

of ten killer whales collected between Kodiak Island, Alaska, and southern California. He found parts of at least three California sea lions, four Steller's sea lions, seven elephant seals, two harbor porpoises, two Dall's porpoises, and one minke whale, in addition to fishes and squids.

When the recorded voices of killer whales were transmitted underwater near migrating gray whales, the grays appeared to be frightened. They swam away from the sound source. Pure-tone sounds and random noise did not bother them.

Zoological evidence tells us that, although killer whales frequently harass larger whales by slashing at their flippers and flukes, they do not often kill one. There are no confirmed records of attacks by the killer upon human swimmers.

Short-finned Pilot Whale (*Globicephala macrorhynchus*)

This big, social dolphin is named from its habit of following a leader or "pilot," usually the largest male in a group. Whalers used to take advantage of its habit to drive pilot whales into shallow waters where they could easily be killed.

When 28 pilot whales ran aground on San Clemente Island, California, three scientists flew to the scene and examined the bodies. Finding no diseases or poisons, they concluded that the whales had followed the leader aground in hot pursuit of squid—their preferred food—then spawning in the shallows.

Record size for males is 20.2 feet (6 m) and about 3.2 tons (2.9 t); for females, 16.8 feet (5 m), weight unrecorded.

Pilot whales range throughout tropical and cool, but not polar, seas of the world. Two species inhabit North American waters— the long-finned pilot whale (*G. melaena*) in the cool temperate Atlantic and the short-finned in warmer waters of both Atlantic and Pacific. Off the Pacific Coast of North America, the pilot whale is seen as far north as the Gulf of Alaska. In the Atlantic, it ranges to Newfoundland.

Navy scientists trained a male pilot whale named Morgan to dive with a grabbing tool clamped onto his beak. Thus Morgan could recover "lost" torpedoes from the sea bottom. Once he dove to the astounding depth of 1,654 feet, surfacing in 13 minutes.

When collectors for an aquarium tried to capture a baby pilot whale, its mother kept pushing the little one away from the capture boat. The baby spouted streams of bubbles from its blowhole. Once landed on deck, it squeaked and chirped continuously, while its mother frantically circled the boat. The men, concluding that the baby was still nursing, restored it unharmed to its mother.

Bimbo, a pilot whale that lived for eight years in Marineland of the Pacific, developed symptoms which, in a person, would be called psychotic. Mercifully he was turned loose at sea.

Harbor Porpoise (*Phocoena phocoena*)

This shy little porpoise, smallest of North American cetaceans, usually is seen at a distance in some secluded harbor as it breaks the surface and quietly blows. *P. phocoena* never approaches a moving ship to sport at the bow wave, and it never leaps clear of the water. Its populations have probably suffered greatly from 20th-century ship traffic, coastal construction projects, and water contamination.

The largest size for both sexes is about 6 feet (1.8 m) and 200 pounds (91 kg). The newborn calf is about 29 inches (74 cm) long and weighs 12 to 16 pounds (5.4 to 7.3 kg). It may live 13 years or longer.

The harbor porpoise ranges from the Arctic Ocean southward along the Pacific Coast to southern California and along the Atlantic Coast to the Delaware River. It frequents cool coastal bays and the mouths of large rivers. Its migrations are more inshore to offshore than north to south.

The harbor porpoise feeds on a wide variety of small fishes and squids, including bottom dwellers. Six porpoises that suffocated in a sea-bass net on the bottom of Morro Bay in California had been feeding in 90 feet of water.

Two men in a boat near the California coast saw an attack by several hundred harbor porpoises on a great school of sardines moving just beneath the surface. Repeatedly, five to seven porpoises would form a rank, side by side, to charge madly through the school. One porpoise might devour as many as a dozen fish in a single rush. Several animals circled the school continuously as though they were "riding herd."

The great white shark (*Carcharodon carcharias*) preys upon the slower harbor porpoise. In the stomach of a one-ton shark caught off eastern Canada were the remains of three porpoises—evidently grabbed from behind, for the tail section of each had been severed by the shark's teeth. A hunter, aiming to shoot a harbor porpoise near the coast of Nova Scotia, was defeated by a 15-foot great white shark. The shark rushed in and bit the porpoise in two, leaving the frustrated hunter with only the head end.

A zoologist who tested a harbor porpoise wrote that its underwater hearing sensitivity was "among the highest ever measured among animals."

Harbor porpoises are seldom displayed in aquariums. They are easily frightened, even though they may have been gently treated for many months.

Some zoologists classify the harbor porpoise and Dall's porpoise in a family separate from the delphinids, partly because these porpoises have spade-shaped rather than conical teeth.

A closely related species (*P. sinus*) lives in the warm waters of the Gulf of California, Mexico, where it is called *vaquita*, Spanish for "little cow."

Dall's Porpoise (*Phocoenoides dalli*)

This handsome, black-and-white porpoise is very often seen in North American waters. Although it lives only in the North Pacific Ocean and adjacent seas, it ranges from the Bering Sea to Baja California. Moreover, it often plays at the bow of a moving ship—racing alongside, seeming at times to dare the pilot to run it down.

During the 1960's and 1970's, Japanese gill-net fishermen in the western North Pacific were accidentally catching and killing an estimated 10,000 Dall's porpoises each year.

The largest male known was 7.2 feet (2.2 m) and 480 pounds (218 kg); females are slightly smaller. The newborn calf is about 39 inches long (99 cm) and 84 pounds (38 kg). The young may be born from June to October.

In the northern part of their range, these porpoises move in spring from the Gulf of Alaska to the Bering Sea and return in the fall. Off southern California, they are most numerous in the fall and winter. They travel in groups of two to 20, though mariners have seen concentrations estimated at 2,000 to 5,000 animals.

The Dall's eats squid and fish, such as saury, hake, herring, jack mackerel, and deep-ocean and bottom fishes.

Although its swimming speed has not yet been timed, the Dall's porpoise may prove to be the swiftest of all small cetaceans. Compared to related dolphins, it has a larger heart, more blood, and greater capacity for holding oxygen in its blood. And in captivity it eats twice as much food as does a bottlenose dolphin of the same weight.

Due to its active, excitable nature, the Dall's had, up to 1965, never been captured and held for more than a few days. Then Navy scientists at Point Mugu, California, succeeded in keeping Marty, a 264-pound (120 kg) male, for 21 months.

The Makah Indians of western Washington called the Dall's porpoise "broken tail," with reference to the large muscle mass on its tail stock. The hump conceivably boosts the animal's speed through the water.

Family Monodontidae

These medium-size cetaceans—the narwhals and white whales—dwell only in the Arctic Ocean and adjacent seas. They lack a dorsal fin, have a small, rounded, beakless head, and have a short mouth cleft that resembles a small smile. The seven neck vertebrae are separate, whereas in dolphins and porpoises (family Delphinidae) some vertebrae are fused. As a consequence, the monodontids have a suggestion of a "neck."

Of all the toothed cetaceans, only the two species represented in this family have become adapted to breeding in water that is chilled by melting ice. They have no counterparts in Antarctica.

In their rigorous environment, they have learned, so to speak, the advantages of sociability. All are gregarious.

Narwhal (*Monodon monoceros*)

The narwhal's common name means "corpse whale" (*nahvalr*) in old Norwegian, from the resemblance of its mottled skin to that of a drowned person.

The male narwhal is unique among cetaceans in having a tooth which continues to grow until it becomes a lancelike, hollow, spiral tusk up to 9 feet long (2.7 m) and weighing 18 pounds (8 kg). Male and female have only two teeth (the upper front), and only in the male does the left one normally become a tusk. It is thought to be a secondary sex characteristic like the antlers of deer, useful in territorial jousting. Once a tusk was found jammed inside the broken shaft of another one, as though two males had rammed each other head on.

The largest male measured was 15.4 feet (5 m) long and 3,528 pounds (1,600 kg); the female 13.1 feet (4 m) and 1,984 pounds (900 kg). The newborn calf, born in summer, is 5 to 5.5 feet (1.5 to 1.7 m) in length. Narwhals live only in the Arctic

Ocean and adjacent seas. Russian scientists based on a drifting ice station saw narwhals within five degrees of the North Pole. In the Canadian Arctic, the largest numbers are seen in Lancaster Sound, in Repulse Bay, off northeastern Baffin Island, and off northern Southampton Island. It is the dream of many a Canadian Eskimo to find a *savssat*, or place where a pod of narwhals has gotten trapped in a bay by sea ice. Here these little whales can easily be taken for use as dog food, human food, lamp oil, and articles of handicraft. One traditional use for the horn of the narwhal male was as material for the *unang*, a light harpoon used in hunting seals. One horn was long enough to make the entire shaft of the implement.

Several thousand narwhals may migrate as a group. In winter, they move ahead of sea ice as far south as Hudson Bay and Labrador. Narwhals in Canada and northwestern Greenland number about 10,000. They are not common in northern Alaska.

They feed on deep-living bottom crustaceans and squid and also take the abundant polar cod and Greenland halibut. Like the other odontocetes, narwhals crush fish between their powerful jaws and swallow without chewing.

In September 1969, the New York Aquarium became the first to exhibit a live narwhal, a calf that lived only a few weeks.

White Whale (*Delphinapterus leucas*)

This, the only all-white cetacean, has been valued for centuries by northern people for its meat, oil, and leather. The newborn calf is brown, gradually paling through shades of gray until, at six or seven years, it turns white.

Docile in captivity, the white whale, or beluga, quickly endears itself. Stefani I. Hewlett, a staff biologist of Vancouver Public Aquarium, reported the exciting birth of the first white whale to be born in captivity and survive for more than a few minutes. Little

Tuaq—Eskimo for "the only one"—arrived headfirst after mother's labor of $3\frac{3}{4}$ hours:

"Brown, with limp little flukes, it swam vigorously and unaided to the surface, popping straight out of the water to past its pectoral fins at least three times. 'Breathe, please, breathe,' prayed Stefani. The baby whale took its first breath on July 13, 1977." It lived 16 weeks.

An adult of record length, 16.4 feet (5 m), weighs 3,528 pounds (1,600 kg). Females are slightly smaller than males. Seventeen newborn calves from Baffin Island had an average

length of 5.2 feet (1.6 m) and weight of 172.6 pounds (78 kg).

Females begin to breed at five years, males at eight years. After mating in May, gestation lasts about $14\frac{1}{2}$ months. Calving often takes place in the warm waters of river estuaries. The calf nurses for a long time—about two years. Growth layers in teeth and jawbones indicate a maximum life span of 30 years.

The beluga ranges as far south as Bristol Bay, Alaska, and the Gulf of St. Lawrence, Canada. It often

ascends rivers and has been seen in the Yukon River 600 miles from salt water. Whites often travel in groups of hundreds. Near Canada's Somerset Island, more than 1,000 individuals have massed at calving time. White whales talk among themselves. Their voices carry above water and are heard by hunters in boats.

At a turn in the St. Lawrence River 60 miles downstream from Quebec, fishermen have caught as many as 320 white whales in a day in the world's only whale trap. It is a seasonal, corral-type structure built of slender poles

Family Physeteridae

A massive forehead and a short, narrow lower jaw give the sperm whales a "chinless" appearance. The spermaceti organ, or case, a unique reservoir of transparent, waxy oil, fills most of the forepart of the head.

The family contains three species—sperm whale, pygmy sperm whale, and dwarf sperm whale—all of which may be seen along the North American coast. The pygmy and dwarf forms (which some authorities place in a separate family, Kogiidae) are not known to exceed 11 and 9 feet (3.4 m and 2.7 m) respectively. Record length for the sperm whale is 61 feet (19 m).

Sperm whales roam the deep waters of all the oceans, though they seldom approach the polar ice fields. Off North America in summer, males are sighted as far north as the Bering Sea and Davis Strait, females and immatures as far north as latitude 50°.

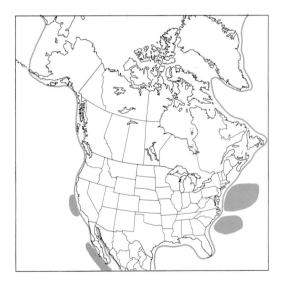

In autumn, both groups migrate southward. Migration routes and areas of concentration are shown on the map.

jammed into the river's bottom. The North American population of whites in recent years was at least 30,000. Of this number 10,000 were regular visitors to Hudson Bay, another 10,000 to Lancaster Sound, Canada, and 10,000 to Alaskan waters.

White whales feed near bottom in shallow waters, where they take salmon, capelin, cisco, pike, char, cod, other fishes, and squid, crustaceans, and sandworms.

Zoologists of the Alaska Fish and Game Department learned that hundreds of white whales habitually gather in the Kvichak River around the first of June each year to gorge on valuable young salmon. So the zoologists placed in the river a powerful sound transmitter which played back the tape-recorded voices of killer whales. When the white whales first heard the sound, they "turned immediately . . . and swam directly out of the river against the strong incoming tide." This system of biocontrol—the control of life with life—quickly became standard procedure.

Sperm Whale (*Physeter catodon*)

When Herman Melville created *Moby Dick*, the story of a bull sperm whale, he could not have chosen a more exciting hero. Fiercely aggressive, outweighing the female more than two to one, the bull sperm earned the fear and respect of small-boat whalers of the 19th century. They learned to their sorrow that he might suddenly turn and attack the ship that brought his tormentors.

The sperm whale is now the most abundant of the great whales, having been hunted with less intensity than the baleen whales.

Worldwide, sperm whales number about 1,500,000. Population may have been 2,000,000 before commercial whaling.

The enormous, box-like head of the sperm whale sets it apart from all other species. The head may contain three or four tons of spermaceti, a substance valued as a lubricant for fine machinery. The blowhole slit is skewed, not positioned at a right angle to the backbone as in beaked whales and dolphins. Moreover, it is on the left side of the head. Small flippers, situated near the rear of the head, could casually be mistaken for external ears. There are 18 to 28 functional teeth on each side of the lower jaws. The upper teeth are few, weak, and non-functional. Most never erupt through the gums.

A male may reach 61 feet (19 m) and 63 tons (57.2 t); the female, 41 feet (12 m) and 26 tons (23.6 t). There have been questionable reports of males up to 69 feet (21 m). The newborn calf measures about 13 feet (4 m) long and weighs about a ton (.9 t).

Sperm whales are polygamous, and individuals group themselves roughly by age and sex. A report of the National Marine Fisheries Service says sperm whales are found "singly or in groups of up to 35 or 40 individuals. Older males are usually solitary except during the breeding season." During the rest of the year large groups may include bachelor bulls (sexually inactive males) or may be "nursery schools"

containing mature females and juveniles of both sexes.

The female matures sexually at 8 to 11 years; the male at about 19 years. Maximum known age is 77 years. The gestation period is 14 to 15 months, and the calf nurses for about 2 years.

The sperm whale feeds mainly on squid, and on octopus and deepwater fishes. Workers at the whaling station at Faial Island, Azores, found in the stomach of a sperm whale the undigested remains of a giant squid weighing 405 pounds (184 kg) and 34.4 feet (10 m) long. Zoologist Robert Clarke, who examined the squid, wrote: "It seems that a whale capable of taking the squid . . . would have little difficulty in swallowing a man, unless it be that a man might slip less easily down the gullet than a mucous-smooth squid."

Off California, wrote whale expert Dale W. Rice, these whales often take roughscale rattails, sablefish, brown cat sharks, longnose skates, lingcod, Pacific hake, rockfish, and king-of-the-salmon (a ribbonfish rather than a true salmon).

By listening through directional hydrophones to the echolocation clicks made by a sperm whale, zoologists tracked the animal to a depth of 8,200 feet. "It seems likely that the depth to which a sperm whale can dive is limited only by the length of time it takes to get down and back," wrote Rice. Two large bulls were shot off Durban, South Africa, in water nearly two miles deep. They had been down 80 minutes and had fresh, bottom-dwelling sharks in their stomachs.

Scientists offer two main theories for the purpose of the spermaceti organ. It may focus and reflect sound. And it may serve as a cooling organ, thus diminishing the whale's volume and its buoyancy during prolonged dives. If the latter theory is true, the animal starts to "blush" as it dives, simultaneously sucking cold water through its right nostril. Cooling the spermaceti only 5.4°F would, in theory, make the body neutrally buoyant.

Family Ziphiidae

These are the beaked whales, diverse in form and habit, exploiting many food niches from the tropics to the polar ice edges. Moderate in size, they have a narrow, tapering snout which, in some of the species, resembles the neck of a bottle. The rear edges of the tail flukes have shallow notches, a distinguishing feature. Beneath the throat are two distinct grooves, which almost meet in front and diverge as they continue onto the chest.

The dorsal fin is small and is positioned near the rear, while the flippers, also small, are positioned low on the underbody. Most beaked whales have only one or two pairs of functional teeth. In the female these are typically buried in the gums. An exception occurs in the rare Shepherd's beaked whale *(Tasmacetus shepherdi)* of the South Pacific, with about 48 pairs.

Whitish, crisscross scratches and scars are commonly seen on the skin of beaked whales of both sexes. Some are tooth marks caused by in-group fighting while others are marks inflicted by squid beaks.

Beaked whales hunt squid and deep-sea fishes which they crush between the lower jaw and the rough, horny palate, the roof of the mouth.

Baird's Beaked Whale *(Berardius bairdii)*

Before shore whaling ended in 1971 on the Pacific Coast of North America, whale hunters would occasionally shoot a Baird's beaked whale as a consolation prize, for this slender whale was considered barely large enough to pay expenses. Canadian whalers at Coal Harbour, British Columbia, used to kill one or two a year; Japanese whalers are still killing about 30 of them a year.

The longest male measured was 39 feet (12 m), and weighed some 13 tons (11.8 t); the female is larger, reaching a record 42 feet (13 m) and about 14 tons (12.7 t). Length of the newborn calf is

about 15 feet (5 m), its weight a little more than a ton.

These whales inhabit the North Pacific region from the Bering Sea southward to Japan and southern California. They travel in tight schools of up to 30 individuals and are wary of approaching ships. Surely they migrate, though the migration pattern is poorly known.

Their food consists of deepwater fishes, squid, and octopus.

Mating is believed to take place in the spring. The calf is born, after a gestation period lasting 17 months, in midwinter.

OVERLEAF: *Trained dolphins dance an aerial ballet in Hawaii's Sea Life Park. In the wild, schools of these exuberant mammals leap and splash for sheer joy—and possibly to signal other dolphins.*

Meat Eaters

Order Carnivora

Survival kit for a young mountain lion—and all carnivores—includes canine teeth specialized to seize and perforate prey. Stalking into close range, it leaps, locking a killing hold on throat or neck.

Wolves and wildcats, bears and weasels. These and many other meat-eaters compose one of the most fascinating orders of mammals, the carnivores. They are the hunting beasts of the animal world. Consisting of some of humankind's closest companions— as well as our fiercest competitors—this order spans a roster of species that have held our attention for centuries.

We can debate forever whether our ancestors' first attitude toward carnivores resulted from fear of becoming their prey, from hate for them as competitors for food, or from appreciation of them as bearers of warm and lustrous furs. Toward a single carnivore, the wolf, one can still see all these attitudes present in humans today—along with a strong social bonding to the wolf's direct domestic descendant, the dog. Myths, legends, fairy tales, and horror stories involving wolves permeate most of the cultures in the Northern Hemisphere, the wolf's original range. And in varying degrees it has been the same with the bears, cougars, weasels, wolverines, and other members of the order.

Not many carnivores can be considered placid. Their need to feed on flesh compels them to dig, scurry, ambush, pounce, bound, lope, climb, or leap. When aroused, they may huff, scream, bark, screech, or howl. Generally they are sleek and strong, quick and alert, their senses finely tuned. Seldom is a carnivore accused of being dull.

Carnivores are a varied lot, with five major groups or families present in North America: the dogs (canids), bears (ursids), raccoons (procyonids), weasels (mustelids), and cats (felids). And they have been a long time in the making. They separated from the ancestors of their prey, the plant-eaters, about a hundred million years ago and have since developed into the animals we know today.

Over time they evolved their own specializations—massive claws in the bears, long-distance communication in wolves, and extreme dexterity in raccoons.

The most distinctive traits common to the members of this order are those associated with their mostly carnivorous diet. Their powerful jaws are specialized for biting and tearing. Their highly differentiated teeth allow efficient butchering and consuming of prey. In most carnivores, the last upper premolar and first lower molar are developed as "carnassials," meat-cutting teeth that scissor past each other to slice tough sinew. Massive molars crush bone, and large pointed canines—fangs—grasp and tear. David Mech, one of the authors of this chapter, once watched a wolf put its fangs to spectacular use in helping its pack capture a large moose. The wolf grabbed the moose by its rubbery nose and held on. The moose raised its head and shook it from side to side, swinging the wolf back and forth in the air. Meanwhile, the other members of the wolf pack kept tearing at the rump of the moose until they pulled their quarry down and finished it off.

After killing its prey, a carnivore is well equipped to make the most of it. In a matter of minutes a large predator tears into its catch and gorges on it. Compared with plant material, flesh is highly digestible. Thus the carnivore's digestive system has a relatively well developed foregut—useful for food storage, digestion, and absorption—and a short hindgut. Its stomach is large and simple. A wolf, for example, can eat almost 20 pounds at a time, and the food is assimilated within a few hours. Several engorgements during the first day after the kill, then, can allow the carnivore to quickly take advantage of what usually is a hard-earned capture. Although carnivores can feast when they make a kill, they often must contend with famine between kills. Several environmental factors affect the number, availability, and vulnerability of prey, and these factors often work against the predator.

After feeding, a carnivore may have to travel many miles and survive many days before locating another animal it can capture. During that time it may lose a great deal of weight. Therefore, the carnivore must try to profit as much as it can from its temporary

A wolverine's dental arsenal typifies that of most carnivores. The upper jaw carries (from left in skull diagram) incisors, a canine, premolars—including the large carnassial—and one molar.

bonanza. Various groups solve the problem in different ways. Members of the dog family bury excess food beneath the ground or snow for later retrieval. Cats and bears protect their kills by scraping leaves and ground detritus over them and returning frequently until the food is eaten. Mech once saw a huge grizzly bear lying completely across a bull moose on which the bear had been feeding. It was hard to imagine anything on earth trying to usurp that animal's food supply.

Weasel family members may hide right with their prey in some cavity or burrow and stay there until all the meat is gone, sometimes for as long as five or six days. The record tells of a fisher—a large member of the weasel family—that found a frozen moose

and began scavenging on the carcass. After hollowing out a cavity in the abdomen of the moose, the fisher took up residence in the hollow. As the carnivore alternated between sleeping and eating, its home grew larger and its larder dwindled. Eventually it ate itself out of house and home.

Just as a carnivore's digestive system and feeding habits are adapted to efficiently process a diet of flesh, so too are its feet adapted to efficiently run down prey animals. Carnivore feet are strong and supportive—even in fluffy snow. Whereas many plant-eating prey animals have sharp, heavy hooves for defense against and escape from carnivores, the meat-eaters have kept the generalized use of most of their toes. This enables their feet to retain flexibility over almost any terrain—muddy areas, fallen timber, or rocky ridges—but still fosters fleetfootedness.

The front feet of most carnivores are reasonably well adapted for food handling. Even in canids, which probably have the least flexible front feet, the paws are useful for holding down bones and small prey while the animal strips or tears chunks of meat from them. The front feet of cats have sharp claws that spring out and puncture prey. Bears possess massive, pointed claws both for hauling down their prey and for digging insects and rodents out of the ground. The front feet of raccoons and weasels are highly flexible, allowing these animals to readily manipulate their prey while feeding.

These physical and behavioral adaptations to a flesh-eating economy would be of little value if carnivores did not have well-adapted senses for finding their prey. Some of the feats of the carnivore sensory system are spectacular. Wolves, for instance, can hear other wolves howling a distance of at least six miles away in forested terrain. Most carnivores can tell in which direction a prey animal has run merely by scenting its trail, which may be several hours old. This means the pursuer can detect minute changes in the scent gradient along the trail, a gradient whose changes result from differences of only a few seconds in the life of the scent. Some dogs can distinguish identical twin human beings by odor and can scent a human fingerprint two to three weeks old.

Most carnivores can see well in the dark because their eyes contain a well developed "tapetum," or reflecting layer, that allows them to utilize light that would otherwise be lost to them. This ability allows cats, for example, to see at a level of illumination only one-sixth of that required by humans.

These superb sensory abilities, the well developed behavioral traits, and the highly specialized physical adaptations make the carnivore an efficient meat-processing animal. But to survive over the millenniums, carnivores also had to learn to heed certain economic rules. It would not pay a mountain lion, for example, to spend several hours hunting a deer mouse. Nor would a weasel be wise to chase a deer.

Instead, each species of carnivore fits into a certain prey niche, taking primarily prey that are of the size, condition, age, density, or living habits that the carnivore is capable of hunting efficiently.

Furthermore, each carnivore species must be adaptable enough to try new strategies whenever necessary or to suspend hunting if circumstances warrant. One wolf pack in Minnesota, for instance, slept four times as much during a winter in which deer were scarce as when they were plentiful.

Not all flesh-eaters are classed as Carnivora. This closely related group of species has counterparts in other mammalian orders: leopard seals of the Pinnipedia, killer whales of the Cetacea. But as a group, members of this order rank among the most typically carnivorous. Hence the name.

Nor are all the carnivores strictly flesh-eaters. Most of them are highly evolved, intelligent opportunists, making the most of whatever food is abundantly available. In addition to mammal flesh—and that of birds, invertebrates, fish, amphibians, reptiles— many of the carnivore species will readily eat many kinds of plants, fruits, nuts, bulbs, or tubers, as well as algae, worms, grubs, and insects. And sometimes carnivores have developed very complicated ways of obtaining their food.

The intricacies of wolf pack cooperation in hunting are legendary. The sea otter actually uses a rock as a tool to open shells of mollusks. Susie, a captive otter used as a subject in Karl Kenyon's long-term study of the species, was given a flat stone along with some unopened clams. A smashing success, Susie grew so fond of the implement she did not let it out of her sight. Later her caretakers found out Susie was also using her pet rock to make more "rocks"—pieces of concrete pounded from the walls of her pool.

Polar bears, the most carnivorous of the North American ursids, are large animals that look cumbersome. But they are both agile and subtle when stalking seals. These bears can pull their ponderous bodies up the steep walls of ice floes or glide silently toward their prey, using irregularities of the ice as cover until they are close enough to strike a blow. When approaching by sea, they can as silently and furtively lower themselves into the water and swim with only a black nose-tip and eyes rippling the surface. Less known is their ability to dive in shallow seas from ice shelves and retrieve kelp from the sea floor. They pick through and eat the kelp.

As a group, carnivores are not only intelligent and able individuals, but they also pass the accumulated "knowledge" of foraging and predation techniques from one to another, especially within family groups or packs. They have, in effect, a highly evolved "cultural inheritance" of great value for exploiting their food resources or surviving in rigorous environments.

The mother bear, for instance, during her long association with her cubs, passes along much information on foraging, the making of dens, and appropriate bear behavior. She is a stern disciplinarian. If a cub does not pay attention, disobeys, or otherwise misbehaves, she may reinforce the lesson with an instructive swat on the rump.

A solitary hunter seizes a morsel—a ground squirrel dug from a burrow. Though grizzlies are able to kill large prey, they mainly subsist on vegetation and carrion as well as small rodents.

Social hunters close in for a kill. As the moose tires from the chase, wolves will attack its rump and sides until it falls. The pack will then gorge on the carcass, leaving only bones, hair, and hoofs.

By the time an individual of the younger generation becomes independent, therefore, it has not only its instinctive abilities but also learned information from its own experiences and information from its mother and from her mother before.

Carnivore populations in any given area are made up of fewer individuals than populations of their plant-eating prey. Meat-eaters must capture and kill what they eat, and when that is consumed, capture and kill again. Obviously they cannot live as densely as their prey species, for they would soon deplete their food resource and perish. And, because of the way carnivores make a living, they must utilize larger areas than plant-eaters do. They must also be able to travel relatively great distances in search of food.

To maintain a population density compatible with food resources, carnivores have evolved social systems that help control their numbers. These systems usually involve some form of territorialism, or spacing out of

A quick red fox pounces—perhaps
on a mouse or gopher. Scent
and sound guide the fox to its
target. The fox leaps—and
pinions the victim with its paws.
Coyotes also employ the tactic.

like animals in a given area. Among wolves and other gregarious carnivores, a pack, or a group of individuals, controls a territory and excludes other packs. Among the solitary carnivores, such as the mountain lion, individuals maintain territories. These territories function as a "home area" or "home range," and each individual or pack usually confines itself to its own area. This spacing limits the overall population of the species and thus averts strife and starvation.

Territories are maintained in different ways. Wolves howl to announce their presence to neighboring packs, and they urinate to leave scent markers at the boundaries of their area. They also aggressively defend their territorial boundaries against invaders—sometimes killing intruding wolves.

Cats use more subtle means of maintaining territories. It is less desirable for them to fight their own kind. A solitary predator must stay in good physical condition in order to survive; badly injured in a fight, it could not fend for itself and would die. Therefore, a more peaceable system for establishing territory has evolved in the cat kingdom. This involves the marking of home ranges with "scrape stations"—piles of earth, pine needles, or similar material scraped together into visible mounds. After scraping up the mound, the cougar may urinate or defecate on it to leave an olfactory as well as a visual sign that the area is occupied. Another cougar, in search of a home, recognizes the sign and moves on. By avoiding each other, the cougars avoid conflict.

Unlike the canids, most cats do not vocalize to maintain their territories. An exception in North America is the jaguar. Because it lives in dense vegetation where sight and scent signs would not work so well, the jaguar cries out to let others know its whereabouts.

These systems among wolves and some cats probably represent a pinnacle in the evolution of carnivore social behavior. Other carnivores have evolved behavior modified to fit their particular needs and life-styles. Bears, for example, eat a wide variety of both animal and vegetable matter. Because the diet of these omnivorous carnivores is not restricted to one type of food, their systems of spacing are less rigid. They often range widely, but if food is plentiful, several bears may remain in a small area for a number of days. When bears congregate, as when brown bears gather to feast on salmon, dominance hierarchies develop to control spacing.

Scent glands are well developed in practically all species of carnivores, and all use scent marking to some degree to advertise their presence. It also seems likely that there is a sexual difference in the scent; thus an individual can recognize whether the scent was deposited by a male or a female.

Size of territories differs widely among the various carnivore species. The least weasel may make use of only a small corner of a woodlot or an unworked area on a farm, while a wolf pack may roam several hundred square miles of northern forest. A bobcat may confine itself to 12 to 15 square miles, while a male mountain lion maintains a year-round territory of 100 square miles. In general, large carnivores depend on large prey animals and cover big areas; small carnivores hunt smaller prey and prowl smaller areas.

There are exceptions. Wolverines are not large—a big one weighs only 50 pounds. But they roam vast areas. One of the reasons for this is their scavenging way of life. To find enough carrion and other food, the wolverine often must travel far and wide. Other species, including the fisher and the lynx, often travel extremely long distances to find their food. Ordinarily these species stay within a definite area. But if they find food becoming scarce, they must move. Wanderings of many miles each day are not uncommon for either the fisher or the lynx.

Reproduction in the carnivores takes varied forms. Mating behavior differs markedly between the gregarious wolves, for example, and the solitary weasels. A dominance order exists in each wolf pack, and normally the dominant male and dominant female mate. When a female weasel comes into estrus, she probably will breed with the first male she meets. Wolf partners remain together as pack members after mating, and the male helps care for the young. Weasel partners part, possibly never to meet again. The female rears the young alone—the usual pattern for most solitary carnivores.

Delayed implantation occurs in bears and most mustelids; that is, the fertilized egg does not implant and grow immediately. A delay of some months is advantageous because young are born at a time when food is more abundant or, for bears, while the mother is wintering in her den. Nearly all carnivores are born quite small and helpless and are cared for solicitously by their mothers.

The period of juvenile dependency for the larger species is long—nearly two years for cougars. But for most mustelids dependency lasts only three to eight months. Most carnivorous species reach sexual maturity in one to two years. Not every sexually mature

individual necessarily breeds. Again social behavior plays a role. If more than one female wolf in a pack should breed, the pack likely could not support all the pups; a single litter has a better chance of survival. When the dominant, or alpha, female dies, the beta female moves up in the hierarchy and subsequently breeds. In this manner the pack can be maintained at an optimum number.

A young female cougar will ordinarily not breed until she is established on a territory. She can better provide food for her offspring when she is on familiar ground and free from the uncertainties of a transient's life. Once more, social structure operates to avoid overpopulation and its dire effects.

Bears, on the other hand, at times control their numbers by killing each other. As population stress builds up, adult males may kill and eat the young—if they can catch them. And pregnant females lose their fertilized eggs if they do not have a certain amount of body fat by denning time. Both of these conditions directly limit bear populations.

Because carnivores kill to live, their effect on populations of prey species has long been debated—often with more heat than objectivity. One of the authors, Maurice Hornocker, has shown, through a long-term study of cougars and their prey, that the cats normally do not decimate herds of deer and elk but help to keep them within the limits of their food resources. Grazing and browsing animals tend to increase in numbers to the point of eating themselves out of food; catastrophic die-offs result. It takes many years to restore the vegetation and, in turn, the animal herds. Predation by cougars tends to lessen the frequency of violent fluctuations in the populations of prey species.

Members of the order Carnivora vary widely in habits and abilities. We must continue to study them and learn from them. We know they are a very adaptable, successful group of species. And they merit all those centuries of our attention.   MAURICE HORNOCKER
CHARLES JONKEL
L. DAVID MECH

Maternal duty and pleasure attain a harmony—an Alaskan brown bear nurses her yearling cubs. Rarely can she take her responsibilities lying down, for she is provider, protector, and tutor-by-example.

Family Canidae

Probably people are more familiar with the Canidae than with any other carnivore family because "man's best friend" is a prominent member of that family. But it cannot be said that the dog is a typical member, because of the great variation among breeds of dogs. Neither the Pomeranian nor Great Dane is a typical canid. The German Shepherd comes closer—most canids have its general body conformation: long legs, narrow snout, large, pointed ears, and long tail. North America's wild canids include foxes, coyotes, and wolves (such as the gray wolf opposite).

Canid feet are especially distinctive. Each has four toes that touch the ground along with a prominent rear pad. This pad is not really a heel, for canids walk on their toes, with their heels high off the ground. This makes for a blocky foot that gives excellent support and allows canids to run swiftly. In larger members of the family, the front feet anchor chunks of prey while the animal strips pieces of flesh and gristle from them. The front feet of all canids also are well adapted for digging soil for dens and for food caches. Claws are thick and hefty, not needle-sharp like those of cats, and are of little use in seizing and holding the prey. The claws function mostly for support of the foot while the animal is running.

As might be expected of animals with feet so well adapted to travel, canids are among the most peripatetic members of the carnivore order. Red foxes have been known to travel a straight-line distance of 245 miles. Wolves may trek 45 miles a day.

Long travel is necessary for canids to find enough prey animals that they can catch. Although most canids will eat a large variety of animal life, and plant matter too, they generally rely on mammals they can run down and catch. They may make many attempts for each successful chase, and they thus must cover considerable ground.

Usually the area hunted by each canid social unit is an exclusive territory. For foxes, a territory may cover a square mile or so; for coyotes, several square miles; and for gray wolf packs, 50 to 5,000 square miles. Canids mark these territories with urine and feces, making "olfactory fences" that keep intruders out. Their voices seem to serve as a supplementary means of maintaining territories. Wolves and coyotes howl, bark, and yap. Foxes yip.

Canid territories are occupied by breeding pairs and their offspring. At least for a given year, pairs are monogamous, a trait rare among mammals, nonexistent in other New World carnivores. Leading to this close monogamous relationship is a prolonged courtship and pair-bonding in which marking with scent seems to play an important role.

Copulation in canids involves another family peculiarity, the copulatory tie. After the preliminaries, the two partners remain tightly locked together for as long as half an hour. The copulatory tie almost seems to symbolize the relationship between the mated pair, for the two remain close partners and both will care for the pups.

A burrow, rock cave, hollow log, or similar location serves as a maternity lair. Canid pairs produce one litter a year, with each litter averaging four to six young—but sometimes more than ten. The pups' eyes open at about two weeks of age, and they begin eating meat at three to four weeks. They are weaned at five to eight weeks. By fall, they are almost full grown.

Fox pups generally disperse to stake out their territories in early fall, coyotes in late fall, and wolves when one to three years old. This means that wolf packs usually contain several members throughout the year, as pups from consecutive litters remain with the breeding pair. Fox and coyote social units generally contain only the breeding pair after the young depart.

Coyote *(Canis latrans)*

"The coyote is a living, breathing allegory of want . . . always poor, out of luck, and friendless. . . . even the fleas would desert him for a velocipede." This assessment by Mark Twain, written mostly tongue-in-cheek, nevertheless does contain some element of truth. Few Westerners have been friends of the coyote. But even its enemies concede its durability. It thrives in the face of all attempts to trap, poison, or blast it to oblivion. This denizen of the Great Plains is expanding its range eastward to the Atlantic, partly because of extirpation of the wolf. New Englanders call it the "coydog" or brush wolf. But it is the same old coyote of lore and legend.

The name coyote comes from the Aztec *coyotl.* Its Latin name means "barking dog." Adults, 2 feet (61 cm) high at the shoulder, are 3.4 to 4.3 feet long (105 to 132 cm) and weigh 20 to 50 pounds (9 to 23 kg).

Tough and wiry, with keen senses and a quick wit, the coyote adapts

readily to almost any habitat. And it is fast—up to 30 miles an hour in a dead run. Coyotes hunt alone (like the mouse stalker above) or team with others to grab a meal. They will eat anything—from rabbits, rodents, and carrion (most of their diet) to watermelons and insects.

Coyotes are monogamous and prolific. The female bears five or six pups each spring; both parents share in their upbringing.

Ten-week-old coyote pups relax at the mouth of their den. Such dens, often remodeled badger holes, may tunnel 30 feet into a hillside.

Calls of the Wild

A Montana coyote fills a frozen morning with its haunting howl. Others howl a response; two or three can sound like a dozen. The wolf shares the howling habit—and so, sometimes, does their housebound cousin the dog.

Why howl? Theories abound, but they share a common premise: To socialize, one must communicate, and howling is communication. Wolves may howl together at dusk to inspire each other, as if with martial music, for the hunt ahead. Perhaps they howl to rally stray members of the pack. Or howling may be an audible "fence" around a pack's territory; hearing it, other packs stay clear and reply with a "fence" of their own.

Using sirens, recordings—even human howls—researchers coax responses from wild canids. Here, taped in the wild and transcribed as musical phrases, are typical howls. They vary as human voices do—from a coyote's brief soprano to a gray wolf's alto. The red wolf's grace notes and inflections produce the most varied melody.

Canids communicate in myriad ways. Some mark their territory with scent posts; a squirt of urine on a tree or rock can tell others the age and sex of each animal that "signs in." Snarls, barks, and growls enrich the vocabulary during closer encounters. A complex body language conveys many meanings.

One wolf flushes a goose, which flees straight into the jaws of a second wolf. Do they communicate on such stratagems? Most experts say no. As with talkative humans, success often takes luck.

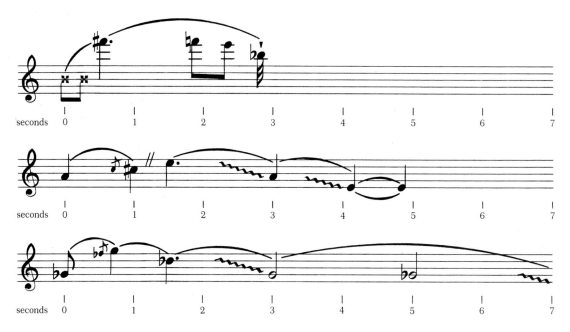

Coyote's howl opens with staccato barks, goes right to its highest note, and ends in a few seconds.

Red wolf's howl builds slowly, hits a melodic high, then trails off evenly.

Gray wolf has the longest howl, a mournful slide from an early high down through an octave or more.

The wolf's life-style requires communication—and thereby hangs a tail. This expressive appendage can send a wide range of messages to other wolves.

Held aloft, the tail asserts its owner's dominance. A tail hanging loosely indicates a wolf relaxed and under no social stress. Slight upward curve may be the beginning of a full-fledged threat.

Tail tucked under signals submission. Wags, twitches, even changes in fullness add subtleties to the rich vocabulary of the tail.

Gray Wolf (*Canis lupus*)

At home in almost any habitat, the gray wolf once numbered 20-odd subspecies throughout the continent. Centuries of trapping, gunning, and poisoning—usually for a bounty—have erased several races and backed the rest into an ecological corner. Some survive in Michigan, Minnesota, and Mexico; others prowl Canada and Alaska. Except for diseases and parasites, the gray wolf's only enemy is man.

Lone wolves are rare; most hunt in packs of a half dozen or more. Gray wolves can lope after a deer, moose, or caribou for miles until the exhausted quarry turns to make a stand. Slashing hooves are often more than a match for the wolves. Only one chase in ten may succeed.

When feeding begins, so do the food fights—mostly bluff, for each wolf knows its place in the pack's hierarchy. At the top reigns the alpha male; to him go the choicest parts. To him also go the duties of leadership in the hunt or in confrontation with intruders. And to him goes the right to mate.

Excitement ripples through the pack at whelping time. All may help to rear the 1 to 11 pups, tending

☐ Present Range
☐ Former Range

them, fetching food, even adopting the orphans if the parents die. An adult may return from a kill with a full gut. Pups nipping at the corners of the adult's mouth may stimulate the older wolf to disgorge a meal for the pups.

Fully grown gray wolves measure 4.5 to 6.5 feet (137 to 198 cm), tails included, and usually weigh 75 to 110 pounds (34 to 50 kg).

The fuzzy pups reach full size in about a year. Then coarse guard hairs cover an underfur so dense that the animal can sleep on snow at minus 40°F.

Gray wolves in Minnesota tussle
in a display of dominance (left).
Yet the winner's hang-dog
tail indicates that this is just
a temporary put-down.

Flattened ears, bared teeth,
raised hackles, and throaty growls
keep the wolf pack's hierarchy
clear as the animals feed on a deer
(below). The dominant male claims
first feeding rights, gulping down
perhaps a fifth of his own weight
in a day. At small kills, others
in the pack may go hungry, but he
stays healthy to lead future hunts
and thus ensure food for all in
the long run. And even a hungry
alpha may fight off other adults
only to defer to a small pup.

Red Wolf (*Canis rufus*)

Arctic Fox (*Alopex lagopus*)

It was the wolf that no one knew. Its home was not the tundra or north woods but the gentle hills and bottomlands of the South. Like a ghost of things long past, it lurked on the edges of our farms and cities through the middle of the 20th century. Then, despite an eleventh-hour surge of sympathy and research, its last wild populations succumbed to a unique process of genetic erosion.

Old specimens, locked away in museums, show that this species once occurred as far north as Pennsylvania and as far west as central Texas. John James Audubon coined its name after seeing some of that color near Austin. In most of its range, it resembled *C. lupus* in color but was smaller: 40 to 75 pounds (18 to 34 kg), with a narrower physique and shorter fur. Its prey, mostly rabbits and rodents, was smaller than that of the gray wolf. So was its home range, about 18 square miles. Pairs established territories, mated in winter, and produced four or five young in the spring.

Human persecution caused a steady contraction of the red wolf's range. Meanwhile, the more prolific coyote pushed in from the west and north, its way opened by human environmental disruption and by elimination of the larger red wolf. As coyote populations expanded, they interbred with and eventually absorbed the scattered, remnant pockets of red wolves.

By 1970 the only pure red wolf population was found along the Gulf Coast in southeastern Texas and southwestern Louisiana. Efforts to save this population failed; the U. S. Fish and Wildlife Service began a Dunkirk-type evacuation. About two dozen were caught and moved to breeding facilities in Tacoma, Washington.

□ Original Range ▨ In 1950
■ In 1930   ▨ In 1970

Attempts at reintroductions in South Carolina give hope that the red wolf may again live wild.

In a lineup of North American foxes, this one would be singled out because of visible adaptations to an arctic climate. Compact body, short legs and muzzle, and small, rounded ears—forms that conserve body heat—mark this polar species.

As winter begins, the arctic fox sheds its brown coat for a thick white one. A minority wears bluish-gray fur in summer, lighter bluish-gray in winter. Day length—not temperature—triggers moult. Active all winter, arctic foxes hole up in a snowbank or den only during severe storms. They feed mostly on lemmings. Probably the widest ranging terrestrial mammals, they will travel more than a thousand miles in search of food. In winter they scavenge polar bear kills on the pack ice. Near the sea they get a seasonal bonanza of fish, seabirds, and their eggs.

Close teamwork helps this fox cope with a precarious, boom-bust environment. Pairs form in late winter and stay together through the vixen's 51- to 57-day gestation. They den under a gravelly mound.

The best den sites are reused and enlarged year after year until the entire mound is honeycombed with tunnels and portals. On top, the fox keeps a watchpost, a place from which to spy out danger or

prey. Large litters, averaging six or more pups, help the species recover from famines brought on by periodic lemming population crashes. Feeding their litter may keep both parents working 19 hours a day.

Red Fox (*Vulpes vulpes*)

Unlike most carnivores, the red fox has expanded in numbers and range since European settlers arrived. It is now the most abundant and widespread fox in North America.

Before settlement, only gray foxes were common in the dense eastern forests. Clearings for farms provided the habitat that red foxes prefer—open spaces bounded by protective stands of trees and brush. The opening of fields also increased the number of voles, mice, and rabbits—all red fox prey.

European settlers also brought a love for fox hunting. Stymied by the gray fox's tree-climbing tactics, they imported European red foxes. Only later was it discovered that red foxes already lived here. Most mammalogists now classify European and American red foxes as one species. Though most bear the golden-red color that inspired their common name, red foxes also come in brown, black, and silver—at times in the same litter. A bushy white-tipped tail accounts for a third or more of the fox's average 42-inch (107-cm) length.

Opportunistic and omnivorous, the red fox eats small mammals, birds and bird eggs, frogs, insects, and berries. In hard times the fox will raid a hen house. Though the farmer may not agree, the fox's value in rodent control offsets the occasional loss of a chicken.

Red foxes are believed to mate for life. In late winter a pair digs a new den or readies an old one— or makes a home in a crevice or cave. Early spring brings a litter of about five. Both parents help raise the young. In the words of zoologist Ernest Walker, "There is no more engaging sight than a litter of fox cubs tumbling and playing about the den, while being watched over by a parent." In early autumn, the family disperses, and each of the young claims its own territory.

OVERLEAF: *Teeth bared, red foxes square off over a meal. Blood is rarely shed in ritualized fights, in which dominance is the big issue.*

Kit Fox (*Vulpes macrotis*)

Swift Fox (*Vulpes velox*)

This perky little fox (here a pup nine weeks old) clearly deserves the name *macrotis*, long-eared. One of its nicknames, desert fox, describes its distribution. Sandy in color, its tail tipped with black, the kit fox dens in loose desert soil. It may either dig its own burrow or borrow one vacated by badger or prairie dog. For quick entry, its refuge may have as many as seven portals.

The kit fox is a small, slender animal. It rarely weighs more than 7 pounds (3.2 kg) or measures more than 32 inches (81 cm) long. The disproportionately large ears are acute sensors of chance or peril in the open desert country. Alerted, the kit fox readily responds. Over short distances it can usually outpace a predator, reaching speeds up to 25 miles an hour.

V. macrotis hunts by night. Using a stalk-and-pounce strategy, it feeds on mice, rats, ground squirrels, birds, lizards, snakes, and insects. Eagles and coyotes prey on it. Ranchers pose an inadvertent threat. Poisoned baits laid out for coyotes are often taken by this canid. Once the kit fox was seriously threatened. But tighter controls on the use of poisons have helped bring it back.

Kit foxes mate in early winter and produce a litter of four to seven in early spring. While the vixen nurses the young, the male provides for her. In two or three months, both parents take the young out to hunt, and the family disperses in autumn.

The swift fox is well suited to its habitat, the high plains of North America. Here the tawny grasses cloak the buff-colored fox. Over flat, open terrain the swift fox can outrun all but the fastest predators. This aptly named fox is as fast as the kit fox, which it resembles in size and weight, as well as general body characteristics. Some mammalogists consider both foxes one species. But smaller ears, a broader skull, and its grassland distribution set the swift fox apart. In western Texas and eastern New Mexico where the ranges of the two species overlap, hybridization may occur.

These foxes breed from December to February. Gestation lasts 50 days and culminates with the birth of two to seven young. The pups emerge from their underground den at three weeks. Soon after, the parents begin showing them how to hunt. The family bond seems strong. If the female dies, the male will raise the pups alone. The young will stay with their parents until the fall.

Small mammals such as rabbits, rats, mice, and squirrels comprise most of this night-hunter's diet. It also eats birds, insects, lizards, and vegetation.

During the first half of the 20th century this species all but disappeared. It often took poisoned

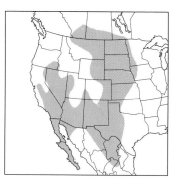

▢ Kit Fox
▢ Swift Fox

bait intended for other animals. The almost total conversion of the prairie to cropland destroyed much of the fox's habitat. Now protected in some states as an endangered species, it seems to be making a comeback.

Gray Fox (*Urocyon cinereoargenteus*)

A gray fox speaks with a canid bark, hoarse and loud. It also has sharp, curved claws and catlike agility—it can scurry up a tree before most people can pronounce the string of Latin syllables that mean, loosely, "gray fox." Silvery gray from long snout to bushy tail topped and tipped with black, the tree-climbing fox measures 32 to 45 inches (81 to 114 cm).

Brushy country, forest, and rocky land suit the gray fox. Rather than dig its own den, this fox may occupy some natural crevice in rocks, a hollow log, or a den left vacant by a red fox or a groundhog. Pups average four to a litter, born in spring. Both parents care for them until they become able foragers.

Not finicky about food, grays take most anything rabbit-size or smaller: rats, birds, lizards, frogs, carrion, corn, nuts, berries, grasshoppers. Even centipedes and scorpions—stingers and all.

Spring flowers garland a gray fox nursery. The pups, about 7 weeks old, will help forage at 12 weeks.

Family Ursidae

The largest carnivores that walk the earth belong to the bear family. One massive male brown bear in coastal Alaska weighed 1,656 pounds (751 kg), a record in the wild. Polar bears rival brown bears in size. There may be a new heavyweight champion roaming a remote corner of the North. But weigh-ins are not part of a polar bear's routine. Polar bear cubs have a head start at birth—24 ounces (680 g) to the brown's 14 (397 g).

The ursid family numbers eight species, three North American: polar bear, black (opposite), and brown, or grizzly. At the subspecies level, and even among individuals of the same subspecies, bears vary so widely in skeletal characteristics that they have been hard to classify. Most bear specialists accept two brown bear subspecies, up to 18 black bear subspecies, and one polar bear race for all of North America.

Bears are stocky, often slow-moving animals with low reproductive rates and overall low population densities. They are intelligent creatures with many learned abilities to utilize food and other resources in a wide variety of habitats. Because their food is only seasonally available, and because most bears den for long periods in winter, they have voracious appetites and must feed almost continuously when their food is abundant. Though diets vary greatly from place to place, vegetation is the mainstay for the black and the brown bears.

Polar bears depend primarily on the ringed seal for food but also eat plants and fish. Bears seek foods high in protein and sugars and are able to extract protein from plants almost as efficiently as herbivores. They can consume huge meals, up to 90 pounds a day for the brown and polar bears. And all three species can gain up to seven pounds in a day.

The eyes and ears of bears, small in relation to their large heads, actually are far keener than most people suppose. Bears also have an acute sense of smell and, in their roaming, often pause to sniff the air—which perhaps accounts for the myth about weak eyes. Bears' lips are free from their gums, an asset in picking berries. Their teeth do not cut and tear as well as those of animals that eat meat exclusively.

Bears have five digits on each foot and have a plantigrade walk: They place the whole foot on the ground. They have strong claws suited to digging out food and dens.

All three species breed in spring, and all have delayed implantation of six to seven months. In late autumn, the partially developed egg implants and final growth starts, perhaps as the female enters her winter den. Cubs are tiny and helpless when born in midwinter and need much maternal care. Fiercely protective of their young, mothers also are strict disciplinarians, teaching their young feeding habits, orientation, and fear of other bears and humans.

Because of their dominance in the wildlife hierarchy, and their generally omnivorous food habits, bears competed with native North Americans and with European settlers for both space and food. And because bears are unpredictable, they posed threats—real and imagined. So people have eradicated them from vast areas of the continent.

Today, with growing numbers of people and shrinking habitats for bears, the competition is more intense than ever. And, though bears are not normally aggressive toward humans, they occasionally do hurt and kill people. Then more bears die.

Long-term studies of bear biology and behavior are vital to holding populations at healthy, productive, yet tolerable levels. Bears can adapt to people and to habitat changes people cause, but they may be near the limit of adaptability in many areas.

These truly wild animals need all the respect, attention—and living space—that sound management can provide.

Black Bear *(Ursus americanus)*

This is the "cute" bear, the teddy, the traffic jammer of national parks from the Great Smokies to the Sierra Nevada . . . the "car clouter" of Yosemite that bashes into cars to get food . . . the "mugger" of the Smokies backcountry that stalks hikers until their nerves snap and they drop their packs and run. This is the one that has dozens of researchers studying how to make the land safe for it—and for the humans whose habits have turned naturally shy bears into muggers, panhandlers, and dump addicts.

Despite human pressures, the black bear still has one of the most extensive ranges of any big animal on the continent. Scientists don't agree on how many subspecies have evolved, but color phases alone suggest numerous gene pools. Some eight to ten subspecies roam the Pacific edge, varying in color from totally black to the pure white Kermodes bear of British Columbia.

In contrast to grizzlies, black bears climb trees easily, pushing off on hind legs, holding with forepaws. They come down in reverse, tail first. Black bears may not look speedy, but they can sprint up to 35 miles an hour.

When fresh scats vanish in bear country, it's a sign the winter sleep has begun. Winter denning varies with the length and severity of the season: six to seven months in Alaska, sometimes not at all in Mexico. Bears den under windfalls, in caves or tree holes (up to 60 feet high in the Smokies). Often they use grass and moss to line their beds and to open and close the entrance for temperature control. A denning bear is said to be dormant; metabolism rate and body temperature do not change sharply, as in true hibernation.

Half-pound (227-g) cubs—usually two, but as many as five—are born in the den. (The triplets above are two months old.) As adults they'll average 300 pounds (136 kg) for males, half that for females.

Black bears are not finicky eaters. Occasionally they rear up on hind legs to sift the breeze for food odors. Carrion? Delicious! Ants will do, or grasshoppers, grasses, acorns, fruits, fish, small mammals, even birds. As climbers, the bears do not have to wait for acorns to drop. In the Smokies they thrash through the tall oaks, leaving the woodland looking as if it had been battered by a storm.

Grizzly Bear (*Ursus arctos*)

"Grizzly" means "grayish" and also "inspiring horror." Both meanings apply. The grizzly's thick, coarse fur varies in color—off-white, tan, yellow, brown, black. In the Rockies the typical hue is dark brown with a grizzly frosting on the back, source of the nickname "silvertip." It is also called the brown bear.

Naturalist George Ord put the second meaning of grizzly into a scientific name (*horribilis*) after reading of Lewis and Clark's adventures with this "tremendous looking animal."

For years *Ursus horribilis* was classed as a North American species; today it is considered a race of the circumpolar brown bear, *U. arctos.*

Most authorities classify our grizzlies and mainland brown bears as one subspecies, *U. a. horribilis*. Another race, *U. a. middendorffi,* called the Kodiak bear, inhabits Kodiak and two nearby islands in the Gulf of Alaska.

Grizzlies average about twice the weight of the black bear, weighing

600 to 800 pounds (272 to 363 kg) as adult males. But size may not offer a good clue to the identity of a lone bear spotted on a distant trail. Where does the bear loom tallest? At the shoulders? The hump of muscle there identifies the grizzly. Farther back, toward the rump? Then it's a black bear.

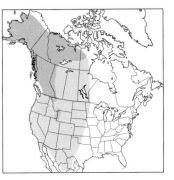

When is a grizzly not a grizzly? When it's coastal—in Alaska. Common usage there applies "grizzly" to inland bears. Those that roam the coasts and islands are called "Alaskan brown bears." Both display the humped shoulder, dished face, and long claws of their species. But at 1,600 pounds (725 kg) the beachcomber above may weigh a third more than the grizzly.

■ Present Range
□ Former Range

Grizzlies mate in late spring. Cubs, usually two weighing about 14 ounces (397 g), are born in the winter den; they stay with mother some 18 months. She becomes sexually active as contact within the family group declines and she leaves the cubs. Or she—or her mate—may even run them off.

Roots, leaves, and berries form the bulk of the diet, but grizzlies also relish meat: squirrel, elk, moose, deer—whether freshly killed or carrion. They feed in garbage dumps and pay the price for eating humans' sugary food: tooth decay. At times they prey on cattle. They avoid humans—but not always, and with tragic results for both.

The grizzly has been eliminated from parts of Canada, Mexico, and the United States. It bestrides the flag of California but is gone from there. South of Canada it has some protection as a threatened species. Even so, it is often shot as a threat to people and livestock.

With habitat loss and the growing human presence in the northern Rockies, grizzly survival even in national parks depends upon research and wise management.

Yet the grizzly remains a force, a symbol of untrammeled nature: "His is a dignity and power," wrote outdoorsman Andy Russell, "matched by no other in the . . . wilderness."

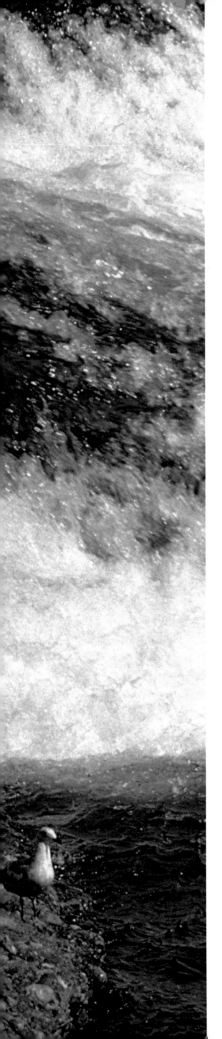

A paw flicks out, pins a fish to the riverbed; jaws snap, securing the catch. Here at McNeil Falls at the base of the Alaska Peninsula, salmon swim upriver to spawn in July and August. They mass at the rapids, as do brown bears of all ages and fishing skills— up to 60 or 80 of them along a hundred-yard stretch.

Brown bears are the most social of our North American ursids. They tend to congregate at food sources and often form family foraging groups with more than one age class of young. Social hierarchies develop as the bears arrive. Biggest males get the best fishing sites. Next come she-bears with cubs, then females without young, sibling groups that stick together, and, finally, the small loners.

240

To make the most of limited fishing space and time at McNeil Falls, the brown bears evolved a stable society that avoids useless combat. A massive, battle-scarred male need not prove himself every time out; the sight of him spooks younger, smaller bears—and he can concentrate on the fish. Dominance bouts often end with open-mouth threats, but not always. One huge male was seen to bite into a 750-pound rival and lift him off the ground. The bloodied loser returned the very next day.

Young bears, such as the ones sparring on these pages, seem to spend their prime time in social play, though roughhousing may lead to a serious scrap.

Protective females start the most fights. For all their closeness, cubs and mothers often get confused about which belongs to which. Several litters may follow a single female; she'll nurse the lot—then let the adoptees choose whether they'll return to their real mother.

With late summer, berry crops lure the brown bears from the river. The social order dissolves, and it's back to the rover's life.

241

Polar Bear (*Ursus maritimus*)

Creature of snow and ice and frigid seas, the polar bear spends much of its time adrift, stalking seals on pack ice and floes. Its white coat—and a body adapted to water— make it seem unique. Actually it is closely related to the brown bear. Mating between the species in zoos has produced fertile offspring, confirming the kinship.

Sizes and weights of the largest polar bears approximate those of the largest brown bears. Adult males may weigh more than 1,200 pounds (544 kg). But they usually are 8 to 11 feet long (2.4 to 3.4 m) and weigh 900 to 1,100 pounds (400 to 500 kg). Females weigh less than half that, and both

males and females are noticeably smaller in the High Arctic than at the southern limits of their range. The polar bear does not have the brown bear's scooped face.

The polar bear's coat, excellent as insulation against the cold, camouflages its hunting activities— and may channel ultraviolet light to its skin. Hairs examined under

A three-month-old cub sticks to its mother in their snowy realm. Polar bears use traditional maternity denning areas where as many as 200 females may gather.

Typically, each digs her den in a snowbank, entering it in October, and adding a chamber as winter drifts deepen. A vent to the surface admits fresh air.

Lethargic during her lying-in, the mother responds with cuddling to the cries of her cubs—usually twins, born November to the end of January. Through the lair's thin dome, increasing light cues the approach of spring. She breaks through the ceiling and emerges, giving her progeny their first peek at the outside world.

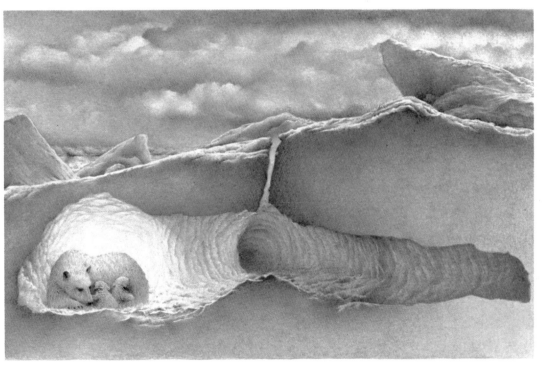

electron microscopes show up as transparent tubes with inner surfaces that reflect light. Thus the white fur may enhance heat absorption. The bear's eye has a well-developed nictitating membrane that acts as a shield to protect the eye from stinging snow and the sun's blinding glare. Polar bears roam great distances

in search of food—but they are not aimless nomads. Their seasonal movements follow definite patterns. Deported garbage-dump raiders unerringly made their way hundreds of miles back to Cape Churchill.

This most carnivorous of the bears subsists in summer on plant foods, birds, and other flesh—including

(above at left) a stranded whale.

In times past, the deep-freeze domain of the ice bear seemed safe from mechanized intrusion. There was a saying: "A polar bear sees a man once in its life—when it is shot." It no longer applies. The race to extract oil and gas from the polar seas encroaches on its range, and concern for this species grows.

OVERLEAF: *Monarchs of the arctic wilds, a female and near-grown cubs clamber onto an ice raft. In their second winter cubs hunt seals with their mothers on the pack ice, denning only during severe storms.*

Family Procyonidae

North America's procyonids—the raccoon, ringtail, and coati—have ringed tails like the one on Davy Crockett's coonskin cap. These species range from the size of a house cat to that of a medium-size dog.

They have extremely well-developed and useful front feet. Each foot has five digits. The animals walk on their toes and at least part of their soles.

Raccoons, ringtails, and coatis are chiefly nocturnal and are excellent climbers. They often rest in trees during the day. Offspring usually are born in tree-trunk cavities. All members of the family are believed to be promiscuous breeders, with males playing little or no role in providing for the young.

Procyonids will eat almost anything: eggs, mice, berries, crayfish, fish, corn, insects, spiders, young rabbits, nuts, fruits. On their nightly forays, they explore just about every nook within their reach. Their dexterity and natural inquisitiveness often lead them to a tasty snack.

Ringtail (*Bassariscus astutus*)

Late at night, after raccoons and striped skunks have eaten their fill and moved on, the ringtail creeps out of its rock crevice to forage. The ringtail has much to choose from in its habitat of desert canyon ledges or brushy slopes. In winter it eats ground squirrels and smaller rodents; in summer, insects, spiders, and desert plants. For this expert climber even the contents of a bird's nest are within easy reach. With a hind foot that swivels 180°, the ringtail ranks among the most dexterous of mammals. In recent years it has extended its range northeastward into Kansas, Arkansas, and Louisiana.

The ringtail resembles many animals, but none closely. Its scientific name means "clever little fox"—its face is foxlike. Its slender body, small feet, and a genius for catching mice gave it many common names ending in "cat." One, miner's cat, dates from gold-rush days when prospectors tamed ringtails for company— and to rid their camps of mice.

The big-eyed, buff-colored ringtail resembles the raccoon most in its bushy, black-banded tail.

An organ of balance, it measures up to 17 inches (43 cm), half the ringtail's overall length. And, arched over the animal's back, it makes the little "cat" appear formidable to possible predators.

Strictly nocturnal and quite shy, the ringtail is rarely seen, though it is not uncommon. Litters of three or four young are born in spring.

Coati (*Nasua nasua*)

The coati's tough, sensitive, and flexible snout has given it at least one nickname: hog-nosed coon. Unlike other procyonids, this one is most active during the day. It is omnivorous—feeding on anything from berries and mice to lizards and insects. (The mother and daughter above examine the prospects for an earthworm dig.) A long, upright tail measuring up to 27 inches (69 cm) equals the coati's body length and often leads people to mistake a coati for a monkey. But this tree climber's tail, though helpful as a balance, cannot be used to grasp.

The rust-colored coati has a dusky face mask and small, soft brown eyes that give it a wistful look. The most gregarious of the procyonids, coatis form casual bands of 4 to 30 or more females and young that live and forage together. An adult male from the group's home range is welcome to join only during the April mating season. Litters of two or more offspring are born in early summer.

The coatis' range reaches from woodlands in Central America and Mexico into the southwestern United States. They crossed the border into Texas about 1900, perhaps as their predators were exterminated.

Raccoon (*Procyon lotor*)

The raccoon, equally at home in city, suburb, or trackless forest, is among the few mammals that thrive in the face of encroaching civilization. It is probably more numerous now in the United States than it was when Captain John Smith explored the New World. It is Canada's only procyonid.

Its diminutive tracks, resembling a human hand in shape, may lead from a hollow tree into mischief. Raccoons are notorious for their nighttime raids on garbage cans. Prying off the lids is no challenge for an animal with thin, mobile fingers and a fine sense of touch. Raccoons kept as pets have learned to turn on faucets, open latches, turn knobs, and manipulate other devices that get them into trouble.

Captive raccoons often douse and "wash" their food in water—a habit that has earned them their Latin name, *lotor*, "washer." No one knows why they do this, but cleanliness is not the reason. Raccoons will also "wash" food—or just their paws—when away from water.

Raccoons measure about 32 inches (81 cm), including tails, and usually weigh about 20 pounds (9 kg). Their litters of two to

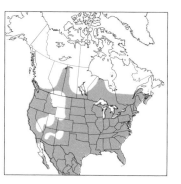

seven young, born in the spring, are raised by the female. A choice den site is a hollow tree 20 to 40 feet up, but any shelter will do.

In winter, northern raccoons become dormant but do not hibernate. A Minnesota trapper entered an old cabin one winter, shined his light about, and beheld a startling sight: 23 pairs of beady eyes steadily staring at him.

Four young raccoons find a hollow tree ideal for playing follow-the-leader. Sprightly and mischievous, they rank among the most playful of mammals.

Young raccoons born in a tree have to climb to the ground before they begin to walk around. How do they do it? Any way they want to—head first or tail first or, as at left, using a two-trunk system. It helps to have hind feet which, if need be, can rotate a full 45°.

Raccoons get plenty of climbing practice. High branches are fine places to sunbathe and to sleep when the raccoon isn't hungry. And when it is—those remarkable paws are good for more than just

climbing. They gave the raccoon its common name. "There is a beast they call Aroughcun," wrote Captain John Smith in 1612 of this New World creature, prized by the Indians for its flesh and its fur. Aroughcun, or raccoon, means "he scratches with his hands."

Seeming never to pause, those sensitive hands scratch, explore, feel, and poke around for food. Rotting tree stumps are a likely place to prospect for termites and ant larvae. No stone, crevice, or even hornet's nest escapes scrutiny. Thick fur protects the coon from stings. Omnivorous, it gains weight rapidly when food is plentiful, storing up fat for the winter.

Swimmers as well as climbers, raccoons can get to delicacies— such as fish, frogs, clams, and crayfish—not accessible to more firmly grounded creatures.

Family Mustelidae

The weasel family is made up of the most diverse species of all the carnivores. It includes badgers and otters, minks and skunks, weasels and fishers. With their differing life-styles, one or more of the mustelids has adapted to virtually every type of terrestrial habitat—underground to treetop—and to aquatic environments, both fresh and salt water.

All have evolved the strong, sharp teeth typical of carnivores. Dependent upon variable and uncertain food resources, they pursue what they need with intelligence and in constantly changing ways. This family, along with canids, felids, and others, arose from the miacids, primitive carnivores of 55 million years ago.

Most mustelids are small, with long slender bodies and dished-in faces. They vary from the cigar-size least weasel to the sea otter, which may weigh up to 100 pounds (45 kg). Their motions are quick if not always graceful, and they possess prodigious strength and endurance. Their legs are short and powerful, and their five-toed feet are adapted for running, digging, climbing, or swimming. Some mustelids walk on their toes, others on their soles as well. Claws are not retractile.

Most mustelids possess anal scent glands, which are used for defense and for marking territory. These glands are best developed in skunks, which rely on scent to ward off enemies. The mechanism is so potent and memorable that skunks often make no attempt to escape enemies. For most carnivores, it is advantageous to blend with their surroundings. But skunks advertise. Their coloration may remind foes they will be sprayed—and forestalls attack. Peaceable, usually in harmony with human aims, the skunk plods about unmolested.

But the wolverine is a mustelid whose behavior and temperament stir enmity whenever it crosses paths with people.

Raiding traplines, wreaking havoc, the wily wolverine has been a competitor to be warred upon and destroyed. Extraordinarily strong, it is perhaps the most tenacious member of a tenacious family. But attitudes toward this wild spirit of the north have changed in parts of its range, and its numbers are increasing in some wilderness areas.

Conversion of vast areas of the continent to farms, highway complexes, reservoirs, cities, and wasteland has harmed most mustelid species, but not all. Skunks profit, for instance, where the pine marten and fisher—forest-loving animals—lose. The badger gains ground where farmland is marginal or reverts to a semi-wild state. The black-footed ferret, a heavy loser, has been all but eliminated.

Many mustelids have the misfortune of possessing very desirable coats. Exploitation of the furbearers varies in intensity as market values of furs rise and fall with the vagaries of fashion, and mustelid population levels are affected accordingly. Trapping has wiped out some species in parts of their range and jeopardized others.

The reproductive potential of mustelids is unusual and widely varied. In most, implantation of the fertilized egg, or blastocyst, is delayed, extending pregnancy to a time of year favorable for birth and survival of young. In the fisher, the result is almost a year of pregnancy. But in the mink, birth takes place about two months after mating. In both species, growth of the young in the womb is of short duration, and they are born poorly developed. Litter sizes in mustelids cover a wide range, from as many as ten for the ermine to only one for the sea otter of the Pacific Coast.

That bewhiskered mustelid (placidly dining on sea urchin opposite) was hunted to the brink of extinction. Given protection, it has made a slow, solid recovery in one of the great conservation success stories.

Marten (*Martes americana*)

Neither deep snow nor the numbing cold of northern winter keeps the marten from its rounds. Frisking over the drifts on furred feet that keep it from sinking in, tunneling beneath when the signs are right, it pokes into every deadfall or sheltered cranny that promises a meal of vole, chipmunk, mouse, hare, or shrew. If action stirs aloft, up it scampers and a branch-to-branch chase ensues. In a marten versus squirrel contest, the carnivore is the odds-on favorite.

Among the mustelids, martens are much more carnivorous than skunks and less so than weasels. Birds' eggs and insects vary the marten's summer diet. When blueberries are ripe, it gets blue lips.

Mature evergreen forests provide habitats suited to this solitary species, also called pine marten or American sable. Each adult animal, the size of a house cat, may need a home range of 15 square miles in times of food scarcity; in times of plenty, only a fraction of that. In addition to the anal scent glands of most mustelids, martens have on their bellies scent glands that are rubbed against the ground to mark territory or to signal the onset of mating season. Females in estrus also use a vocal signal: They cluck. After potential mates meet, a reluctant female may be dragged by the scruff of the neck until she

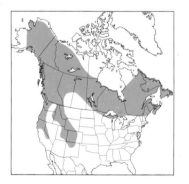

cooperates. Her young number two to four and arrive in early spring.

Loss of habitat from logging, fire, and spreading humanity has robbed the wilderness-loving marten of many former homes.

Its intense curiosity makes this beautifully furred animal an easy mark for trappers. Almost any bait, edible or not, will work. And some martens never do learn. Biologists studying the species in Glacier National Park live-trapped one hyperinquisitive male 77 times.

The snap of a trap is usually the sad end of a tale—but not always. Some martens taken in traps of a non-lethal sort are being transplanted to logged-over forests that have regrown—in the hope new populations will flourish.

Fisher (*Martes pennanti*)

The fisher does not fish for a living. Instead, this close relative of the marten is known for its speed through the treetops. Wrote naturalist Ernest Thompson Seton, "It is probably our most active arboreal animal. The squirrel is considered a marvel of nimbleness, but the marten can catch the squirrel, and the fisher can catch the marten."

A fisher sometimes does catch and eat a marten but more often it feeds on hares, small rodents, birds, carrion, and fruit. Where its range overlaps the marten's and they compete for food, the two may specialize by size, the larger fisher taking larger prey.

With a unique degree of success the fisher makes a food resource of the well-armed and populous porcupine. For a long time it was thought the fisher's technique involved upending the lumbering rodent and attacking the flip side, which lacks quills. Not so, studies show. The porcupine's defense works best against attack from above and behind. The fisher's low profile puts it at the right level for a frontal attack, and it uses teeth and claws to inflict wounds on the porcupine's face and neck before tearing into its belly.

Because too many porcupines can debark and kill too many trees, foresters and fishers have become allies in parts of former fisher habitat—in Montana, Idaho, Oregon, Vermont, Michigan, Wisconsin, and West Virginia. Finding a few hungry fishers more desirable than buckets of poison, wildlife

managers have restocked the deep-woods predator to kill off excess porcupines and save trees.

At home in the wilderness, the fisher finds a hollow tree or log a fit den for its slim body—up to 25 inches (64 cm) long, excluding the tail. The one to five young are born in March or April and become independent by fall.

A female fisher mates a week or so after bearing young, then undergoes a gestation period of up to 358 days. Of this, ten months pass before the embryo becomes implanted; its actual development takes about two months. Thus, in a sense, the female spends nearly all her adult life in a state of pregnancy.

Ermine *(Mustela erminea)*

Long, slender skulls and sinuous bodies fit the weasels for their niche in life: They are a scourge of small burrowers, such as mice, voles, moles, and chipmunks. Weasels can enter any burrow or hole they can get their heads into.

In the open, a weasel stalks chiefly by scent. In lightninglike moves it pounces on its prey with clawed forelegs and kills it with bites to the back of the neck. Weasels can kill rats, rabbits, and squirrels larger than themselves.

Middle-sized among the three weasel species in North America, the ermine weighs 1.6 to 3.7 ounces (45 to 105 g) and is 7.5 to 13 inches (19 to 34 cm) long. About a third is tail, giving the ermine another common name, short-tailed weasel (though the least weasel's tail is even shorter). The ermine in North America ranges from northern states to above the Arctic Circle. Weasels are bolder than their small size warrants. On occasion they have attacked humans who stood between them and their food.

Captive weasels eat a third or more of their weight each day. Seldom does nature provide a steady source of food. So the weasel's mode of survival is to kill whatever it can whenever it can and store the surplus. Its den often has a side tunnel used as a storeroom for slain mice.

Confronted with an unnatural surfeit of food, as in a farmer's hen house, the voracious ermine follows the only pattern it knows—and overkills.

The ermine breeds in early summer. After delayed implantation, four to ten young are born in the spring.

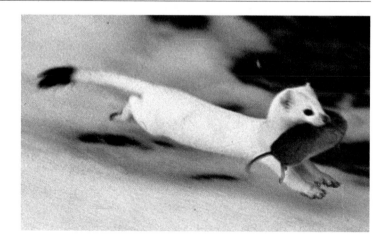

Ermine in winter pelage spirits away a vole. Brown in summer, the weasel wears white in winter. Blending with the season, it benefits as hunter and hunted. The tip of its tail remains dark.

A predator, seeing only the spot of color moving against the snow, may strike behind it.

Long-tailed Weasel (*Mustela frenata*)

This largest of North American weasels weighs 2.5 to 9.4 ounces (72 to 267 g), is 12 to 22 inches (30 to 55 cm) long, including a 4- to 6-inch (10- to 15-cm) tail. Found from Peru to Canada, it has a range that overlaps those of the ermine and the least weasel.

The presence of three similar carnivores in an area, feeding on essentially the same prey, is unusual. But this weasel's size enables it to kill larger prey, thus helping assure all three species adequate food. Coyotes, foxes, hawks, and owls that prey on all three weasels reduce the populations of each and ease competition for the same food.

In the northern part of its range the longtail, like the other two weasels, changes color from dark brown to white in autumn. (Pelage of the ermine—opposite, top— is in the process of change.) As the days grow shorter, less light enters the weasel's body through its eyes, stimulating moult by means of the pituitary. This gland also inhibits release of pigment to the cells in the hair follicles, resulting in a color change as the pelage regrows. A second moult as the days grow longer reverses the color scheme.

As persistent and fearless a hunter as its fellow weasels, the longtail is also equally adept at climbing and swimming. It seems to prefer more open habitat.

Breeding in midsummer, the longtail bears three to nine young in the spring, implantation having been delayed about eight months. The new generation reaches maturity within six months, and females are able to mate in their first year of life.

Least Weasel (*Mustela nivalis*)

The world's smallest carnivore, the least weasel may weigh less than an ounce and hardly tops 2 ounces (28 to 57 g). It is at most 9.8 inches (25 cm) long, about a quarter of that tail (not black-tipped, as on other weasels).

A high metabolic rate drives the least weasel constantly in search of mice, its principal quarry. A rise or fall in mouse population may have a similar effect on weasel numbers. Like other weasels, it often usurps a victim's burrow and uses it as a base for more forays. To prepare the den as a nursery, the female may line it with the victim's fur.

Least weasels do not experience delayed implantation. Thus, they can produce two litters a year. Litter sizes vary from three to ten.

Speed, ferocity, and the ability to crawl into tight spaces help it cope with an array of predators. As a last resort, the least weasel can emit an odor said to be as pungent as that of the striped skunk, though it cannot spray the musk as skunks do.

Black-footed Ferret (*Mustela nigripes*)

Mink (*Mustela vison*)

The black-footed ferret, probably never abundant on the plains of North America, now is in danger of vanishing altogether. Little is known about this black-masked marauder in a tawny coat. Even its existence went unrecognized by scientists until 1851, when John James Audubon and John Bachman described it from a skin provided by a trapper. Today it ranks as the continent's rarest mammal.

Active mainly at night and at dawn, the ferret depends heavily on the prairie dog for food and shelter. Originally, the ranges of the two species coincided: from Texas north across the grasslands into Alberta and Saskatchewan. But cattle ranchers, seeing the prairie dog as a competing grazer, launched massive campaigns to wipe it out. And in this war the ferret's habitat was disrupted.

Ferrets may also prey on mice, ground squirrels, and gophers. But prairie dogs are the ferret's chief food. The ferret hunts mostly underground, within the prairie dog's labyrinthine passageways. The ferret seizes a victim by the throat, kills it, and drags it out to the ferret's burrow. Prairie dogs show little or no fear of the ferret above ground. Below ground, they may try to keep a ferret in or out of a tunnel by plugging it with dirt—a strategy that apparently seldom succeeds.

To feed herself and an average litter of four, a female ferret would need, by one estimate, a larder consisting of a prairie-dog town covering at least 15 acres.

Ferret young are born in the spring. In summer, the mother takes them above ground, usually at night. In the fall, the young disperse to lead solitary lives. At full growth, they will measure about 22 inches (56 cm) nose to tail, and weigh 2 or 3 pounds (0.9 or 1.4 kg).

Elegant in its lustrous brown coat, a mink slinks from its riverbank den. It was a muskrat's den, until the mink killed and ate the owner. Hungry again, always hungry, the mink embarks on another foray. All night and at times by day, in the water and on land, this close kin of the aggressive weasels prowls—alone. Except briefly at breeding time, a mink will not live in a place crowded with others of its kind, even though food is plentiful.

The mink climbs well and, having semi-webbed feet, swims well, the rich fur protecting its streamlined body from icy water. An amphibious mode of living puts great variety into the list of possible prey, including fish and crayfish. One food study in a North Dakota prairie marsh tallied 32 species of prey identified from mink scats and uneaten remains in and around their dens. Dabbling and diving ducks, blackbirds, frogs, and garter snakes were among the kills, as well as the voles, mice, and shrews that are weasel staples. The versatile mink may be found from Florida into the Arctic, in all but very dry areas.

The litter of two to ten kits, born in spring, receives tender care. The family may change dens several times before the kits mature and disperse. Minks measure up to 28 inches (71 cm) including tail, and weigh up to 3.5 pounds (1.6 kg).

Large owls, bobcats, coyotes, and human trappers prey on minks. Commercial ranches supply most of the demand for pelts. As many as 100 are needed to make one full-length coat.

Wolverine (*Gulo gulo*)

Legendary "devil beast" of tundra and boreal forest, the wolverine is probably unexcelled in strength by any mammal its size. This giant weasel, bearlike in shape, measures 36 to 44 inches (91 to 112 cm) from nose to tail tip. It weighs at most 50 pounds (23 kg). Yet it has chewed through and pulled down logs a foot thick to rob a trapper's food cache and has killed moose 20 times its size. Usually when an outsize animal becomes wolverine fare, it is old, weak, hampered by deep snow, or already dead. A wolverine will eat as much as it can hold of anything it can get.

Winter is a time of hunger for many arctic animals, but the wolverine does not migrate or hibernate. Mastery of snow travel aids in making a living. Broad, furred feet spread the weight of this formidable snow mammal, letting it lope over crusts. It may cover 30 miles a day to find prey or scavenge kills of other predators, including humans. Wolverines are notoriously adept at working traplines. They not only eat the meat but may carry away the traps. Occasionally, they scent-brand

food they have no immediate use for. The elusive wolverine is better known by its works and its odor than by sight.

In a den under the snow or other sheltered place, two to five young are born from January to April. They grow rapidly and are on their own by the following winter.

Traps and poisons, along with loss of habitat, almost wiped out the wolverine in the United States. In many states laws now protect it, and its survival seems assured.

☐ Present Range
☐ Former Range

Badger (*Taxidea taxus*)

The scene of a badger's life story keeps shifting from one hole in the ground to another. Born and bred in a burrow, it spends a good part of its time digging in and crawling out. In summer it may go through a den a day, not sleeping in the same place two days in succession. In cooler weather a longer tenancy is usual. If it digs up a big meal, such as a rabbit, the badger may drag its kill into a tunnel and hole up for several days. The usual fare is smaller—ground squirrels, mice, snakes, bees—and every day is the same old story: dig, dig, dig.

This resident of arid grasslands and sagebrush country digs not only to eat, rest, and nest, but also to bury its feces and to take refuge from belligerent farm dogs.

Badgers have a body shaped for life underground—short and flat. The animal can flatten its body to wriggle and crawl through a network of burrows. Its legs are short. Its long, strong claws are designed for digging. These, combined with the badger's ability to shove loose earth with its body, make it the most prodigious burrower among carnivores. It measures up to 34 inches (86 cm), including tail, and weighs up to 22 pounds (10 kg).

It may live close to humans but shuns contact with them. Its burrows can be a problem on farms,

and cowboys have always regarded badger holes as hazards for horses

When cornered, badgers fight fiercely, and men once trapped and baited them for sport. They would put one in an open barrel or similar place and force it to fight against dogs. The badger would back into its corner and, growling and snarling, face its tormentors. From the cruel sport of baiting badgers came our usage of "badger"—to harass and worry.

An adult badger normally wanders alone except at mating time. When a female has her one to five cubs, she settles in one burrow for about a month, until the young can venture out with her and seek another home on the range—and another and another.

Striped Skunk (*Mephitis mephitis*)

Turning its back to the enemy, arching its spine, and lifting its tail, the striped skunk sprays an oily, foul-smelling fluid up to 15 feet away. The odor can travel half a mile on the wind.

Most mustelid species have well-developed scent glands. But in *M. mephitis* and other skunks, this trait has evolved into an important means of survival. Two glands located at the base of the tail contain about three teaspoonsful of musk, enough for five or six discharges. The skunk can replace this fluid at a rate of about two teaspoonsful a week. Spraying is the ultimate response to danger, and warning signals usually precede its use: hisses, growls, foot-stamping, tail-waving. Though rarely used, the chemical defense is so effective that the skunk's name and reputation derive from it. *Mephitis* means "bad odor."

This creature is peaceable, plodding, and all but harmless if left alone. Black, with a distinctive forked stripe along its back, it is the most common skunk in North America. It occurs from Canada's Northwest Territories to central Mexico. Preferring fields over forests, it has adapted well to human alterations of the land. Although it generally inhabits natural crevices or dens abandoned by other animals, it also lives under buildings, in woodpiles, or around garbage dumps. An omnivore, it eats vegetable foods, grubs, insects, mice, shrews, eggs, and carrion. In total length, males measure 23 to 31.5 inches (58 to 80 cm). Females are somewhat smaller.

A pleasant sight of late springtime is a skunk parade along the roadside, a mother with her four to seven kits following single file, out for an evening stroll and a meal. Used to getting the right of way, skunks have poor road sense, and traffic takes an odoriferous toll.

Striped skunks have few predators. Humans shoot or trap them. Bobcats attack on occasion. So does the great horned owl, which has better eyesight than sense of smell.

Hooded Skunk (*Mephitis macroura*)

Markedly hairy at each end, this skunk is well named—in two languages. Longer hairs around the neck resemble a hood; *macroura* means long-tailed. That bushy appendage accounts for half the skunk's total length, 26 inches (66 cm). Some hooded skunks are almost totally black; others are well streaked with white.

This species lives in deserts of Mexico, southern Arizona and New Mexico, and western Texas. In streamside brushlands and rocky canyons it forages for insects— the mainstay of its diet—and small rodents, bird eggs, and plant foods. It serves as an important check on the populations of large insects and small rodents that thrive in the year-round mild climate of its homeland. Very little is known about the hooded skunk; its manner of living is probably similar to that of the striped skunk. Its dens most often are found in rocky crevices or dug into the soil. Unlike the striped skunk, this one seldom lives in abandoned cabins or under sheds.

One litter is born each year, probably containing three to five young. The species is nocturnal and, except for an occasional coyote or bobcat, is seldom preyed upon.

Hog-nosed Skunk *(Conepatus mesoleucus)*

Spotted Skunk *(Spilogale putorius)*

With its bare, flexible snout the hog-nosed skunk roots for insects, grubs, and worms in desert valleys and brushy canyons of Mexico and the southwestern United States. Sturdy claws on its forelegs aid the quest. Its diggings look much like the work of hogs. The hog-nosed skunk also eats small rodents, reptiles, and vegetation, including prickly-pear cactus fruit.

Little is known of this species' reproductive behavior. A litter of two to four young is born in spring after a gestation period of about two months. The adult hognose weighs between 3.4 and 10 pounds (1.5 to 4.5 kg) and measures 23 to 27 inches (58 to 69 cm).

Nocturnal and solitary, it is seldom seen foraging. When met, it pays an onlooker little heed.

Head down, intent on rummaging through the soil for food, it seems to fear no predator. Trappers do not value its coarse, brown-tinged fur. Its musk can send even rattlesnakes wriggling away.

Conepatus, "little fox," is South America's only skunk genus, and only *C. mesoleucus* ranges into the United States. It reaches as far north as Colorado, where it is never abundant. The hognose is threatened by civilization's advance into the desert, especially into less arid canyon bottoms, where loamy soil supports enough insects to sustain the skunk.

The smallest North American skunk is distinguished by its coat, a silky collage of spots and broken white stripes. Adults are about 20 inches long (51 cm) and weigh about 2 pounds (0.9 kg). Spotted skunks are adept at clambering up trees—and occasionally live in them. More often, they den underground. Small size and the ability to climb enable this species to steal into hen houses more easily than other skunks. Though fond of eggs, they usually eat rodents, insects, snakes, and fruit. Owls, foxes, and bobcats sometimes prey on them.

Spilogale putorius—roughly translated, "spotted stinker"—ranges from British Columbia to Central America, though it is absent from much of the northern United States. It bears a litter of two to six in the spring.

Fair warning says the artful handstand and waving tail of a spotted skunk. If the enemy comes closer, it gets sprayed.

River Otter (*Lutra canadensis*)

The engaging river otter cavorts in and out of water through most of the United States and Canada, appearing to enjoy life thoroughly. It can live near people and seems to like showing off for an audience.

The otter's lithe, streamlined body, with short legs and webbed feet, enables it to swim at speeds reaching seven miles an hour.

Adults are as long as 51 inches (130 cm), including the fleshy, tapered tail that serves as a prop on land, a rudder or oar in water.

Otters mate in the water, usually in winter or early spring. Male and female then go their separate ways. One to five pups are born nearly a year later in a riverbank den the female prepares—perhaps after evicting a muskrat or beaver. At about 12 weeks, the young venture out of the den. Soon they are swimming and expertly hunting their favorite foods—fish, crayfish, frogs, insects, and small mammals.

Rhythmic as a ripple, the otter dives and surfaces, undulating through the water by flexing its body up and down. Watch a "train" of otters snake down the middle of a river and you may think you're seeing a sea serpent of monstrous size. (You won't be the first.) This adept aquanaut can easily dive to 35 feet. Flaps of skin close its nose and ears and its pulse rate slows, allowing it two minutes underwater before it must pop up for air.

Agility and speed in the water come in handy not only for catching fish but also for catching pebbles tossed in a one-otter game of ball—or for strategic withdrawal after a teasing tug on a beaver's tail.

Body-sledding down a snowbank is another favorite activity. Otters go as a family group. Adults take turns with the young at tobogganing on their bellies. When there is no snow, a slippery mudbank will do, preferably angled to the river so the slide can end in a resounding belly flop.

Sea Otter *(Enhydra lutris)*

Lolling on a kelp bed along the Pacific Coast, shielded from frigid water by luxurious fur, the sea otter seems to lead an easy life.

Its ancestors once lived on land. After taking to the sea eons ago, they did not develop a blubbery layer beneath the skin, as whales did. The otter depends for protection from the cold on the blanket of air trapped in its densely packed fur, a fur so fine it almost doomed the species.

Said Captain James Cook after acquiring some pelts from Nootka Indians in 1778: "The fur of these animals . . . is certainly softer and finer than that of any others we know of." Sea otters were already being killed for their pelts by Europeans, Asians, and North Americans. Cook, China-bound, took furs with him. The demand and the slaughter grew. The fur trade nearly wiped out the species.

In 1911 the United States, Great Britain, Russia, and Japan agreed to stop the killing. The near-shore animal has made a substantial comeback in the Aleutian Islands and off the California coast south of Monterey. It shows promise where it has been transplanted.

The sea otter, 4 to 6 feet long (122 to 183 cm), usually weighs 33 to 66 pounds (15 to 30 kg), but it may reach 100 pounds (45 kg). The male is the largest North American mustelid. Females are about 20 percent smaller.

Adults first breed at about four years, courting and mating in the water. A single pup—rarely two—is born six to eight months later. With no margin for error in a litter of one, the newborn is better developed than most mustelid pups, arriving eyes-open with a mouthful of milk teeth. For a year the pup will nurse, nap, and be groomed. Its mother will carry it on her chest while she floats or swims on her back. Males usually live apart.

Grooming is not a mere nicety. If the otter's coat—containing some 800,000,000 fibers—gets soiled or matted, the trapped air is lost and with it buoyancy and insulation. Oil spills and other pollution—and competition with commercial fishermen for some of its favorite foods—are among the problems that still menace the otter.

A dive to the bottom puts a large abalone within this successful hunter's grasp (left). Sea otters bring their food to the surface to eat, hauling it up in a pouchlike chest fold or clasping it with prehensile flippers. They may dive as deep as 180 feet to find edibles—chiefly mollusks, crabs, and sea urchins—and may eat a fifth of their body weight in food each day. The otter above uses a rock balanced on its chest as an "anvil" to batter open a clam.

Family Felidae

The cats are the most lithe and graceful of all the mammals. And, of all the carnivores, cats are perhaps the most proficient killers. Members of this family possess keen senses and lean, muscular bodies ideally adapted for a predatory existence. Forelimbs are armed with sharp claws. Longer hind limbs provide for amazing leaps and bursts of

are purring cats and are members of *Felis,* although many modern authorities assign the bobcat and lynx to the genus *Lynx.*

In both form and function cats reach the peak of predatory evolution. The teeth, fewest in number among carnivore families, are also the most specialized. The canines are better developed for seizing and perforating prey than those of any other flesh-eater. Even the tongue is specialized. It is covered with sharp, horny protuberances which rasp meat from bones. The tongue also is effective in grooming the animal's coat, which is one reason cats look so sleek.

Outwardly, all cats appear very "catlike." Their coat colors differ. The jaguarundi and cougar (opposite) have plain coats; others are spotted. In each case, the fur acts as camouflage, an asset to a hunting species.

Solitary and secretive, cats usually live in inaccessible rocky terrain or dense cover. Relying on stealth to catch prey, the felids stalk, then spring upon any prey they can overpower and kill—mammals, birds, fish, even reptiles. Seldom do they wait in ambush for prey to come to them. They usually inflict killing wounds with bites to the neck or throat of larger prey; smaller prey are crushed in the jaws.

Of all carnivores, cats have the largest and perhaps sharpest eyes, directed forward in the skull, befitting a hunter. Cats generally are nocturnal, and their night vision is well developed. The senses of hearing and smell are probably less acute than in canids.

The cats shun human contact, and, though some attacks have been documented, people have little to fear. Research has shown that cat predation on deer and elk helps to keep these herds within the limits of their food resources. Such new knowledge and an increased appreciation for all wildlife give hope that an enlightened human society will provide for the continued existence of the spectacular animals called wild cats.

Cats bare five long, curved claws to grasp prey or rip at an enemy. When not in use, the talons retract into sheaths to protect the sharp points. Furred feet of the felids permit a soft and noiseless tread.

speed. Jaws and teeth are designed to seize, kill, and devour other animals. Some cat species are capable of killing prey far larger than themselves. The felids are among nature's finest physical machines.

Taxonomically, the cats of the world are divided into *Panthera,* the large roaring cats, and *Felis,* the smaller purring cats. Because of the different way the voice box is attached, the members of *Panthera* rasp or roar in deep, gruff tones; members of *Felis* purr continuously or make shrill, higher pitched sounds. Of the seven cat species found in North America, only the jaguar belongs to the genus *Panthera.* The other six—mountain lion (or cougar), lynx, bobcat, margay, ocelot, and jaguarundi—

Mountain Lion (*Felis concolor*)

Mountain lions, or cougars, do not stalk about "screaming." If they did, they would scare prey animals away and go hungry. Nor does the cougar roar. It makes many sounds similar to those of house cats, but louder. A set of whistlelike sounds—studied in captive cougars—may be used by wild pairs or in families to call and warn each other.

Also called puma, panther, or catamount (cat of the mountains), the mountain lion is the largest of the North American purring cats. Adult males weigh 148 to 227 pounds (67 to 103 kg) and measure 5.6 to 9 feet (171 to 274 cm) from nose to tail tip.

Mountain lions are strict loners. Adult males and females show social tolerance only during the two-week breeding period, and females and young during the long juvenile dependency period. Breeding is not confined to any one season, but in the northern parts of their range cougars breed mostly in winter and early spring. A pair will remain together for the two weeks, perhaps longer. Then they part, and the male plays no further role in the family.

One to six spotted kittens are born after a 90-day gestation period. The spots will give way to the uniform coat of russet or tan responsible for the species name, *concolor*, "uniform color." Kittens are born in a cave or other sheltered place, as under a rock ledge or windfall. Helpless at first, they grow rapidly. The mother brings meat to them in addition to providing milk. After about two months they leave the home den and live in temporary dens and caves while the mother hunts for food.

The young lions possess certain inherent abilities as predators. But they also need to learn, under their mother's tutelage, techniques for killing such large prey as elk.

The neck muscles of an elk are too thick for a cougar's bite to be fatal. By using their forelimbs to twist and snap the elk's neck, cougars in the central and northern Rocky Mountains sometimes kill elk five or six times a cat's weight.

Its training complete at about 18 to 22 months of age, each young lion soon goes its own way.

The cougar once ranged from coast to coast and from central British Columbia to South America. It now occurs in significant numbers only in the areas shown on the map.

Biting venison from a kill, a lion uses carnassials, special cheek teeth that scissor the meat.

OVERLEAF: *A blur of speed, a cougar streaks from pursuers. The shy, secretive cats lead solitary lives.*

Ocelot (*Felis pardalis*)

Garbed to blend into their dappled sun-and-shadow world, ocelots wear beautifully marked coats. And the coats made them marked animals. They and other spotted southern cats were heavily hunted. But the Endangered Species Act made importation of their furs illegal in the United States. Some Latin American countries also officially protect these rare cats.

At home in forest and brushland, ocelots usually rest by day hidden in foliage and at night hunt small and medium-size prey: rabbits, birds, monkeys, pacas, agoutis, iguanas, fish, and frogs. A male and female sometimes roam together.

An adept climber, the ocelot may tree when pursued, though, wrote Ernest Thompson Seton, "He can run like a fox, can blind-hop, back-track, and double-cross his trail." Mexicans who hunted ocelots when they were more abundant not only took the pelts but also consumed the meat and blood. Traditionally, such fare had extraordinary power to abet strength and health.

In cooler parts of their range ocelots tend to bear their young in spring; in tropical areas births may occur in other seasons. A cave or hollow tree may serve as a den.

Information on the elusive species is limited. An average litter is probably two or three.

An ocelot is 36 to 54 inches (92 to 137 cm) long, including a tail of 11 to 16 inches (27 to 40 cm).

Margay *(Felis wiedii)*

Almost a copycat, the margay looks like a small-scale ocelot. Its total length is 32 to 51 inches (81 to 130 cm), including a tail of 13 to 20 inches (33 to 51 cm).

Nearly all that is known about this eye-appealing felid has been gleaned from captive animals. A superb aerialist, the margay likes to climb up to and leap from high perches even when there is no prey for it to pounce upon.

Transferred to a forest setting in Mexico or Central America, such gymnastics would suggest a margay diet of rodents, rabbits, and birds, for its hunting operation can shift effortlessly from tree limb to the ground. The margay's range limit is tenuously put northward into Texas on the basis of a single animal found at Eagle Pass on the Rio Grande a century ago. But the supersecretive habits of this very rare cat may, in part, account for the scarcity of sightings. It is presumed to be nocturnal.

By day, the pupils of its large dark eyes, like those of most other small cats, narrow to vertical slits.

Among other common names, the little "tiger cat" is called *chulul* by Mayans of Yucatan, and *pichigueta* in Chiapas, Mexico.

Jaguarundi (*Felis yagouaroundi*)

Hued like the desert dusk, the elongated, low-slung jaguarundi can stalk unseen in the half-light. Twilight and dusk are its most successful hunting times. This small-headed southern felid in contour resembles the weasels about as much as it does fellow cats. Tail down, it moves sinuously through the barbed brush called chaparral with scarcely a ripple of leaf or twig to betray its presence. Eventually its body

tenses. One pounce, and a bird in the bush is a bird consumed.

Though an agile climber, this species spends less time in trees than the ocelot. Rodents, other small mammals, and fish from the streams vary the jaguarundi's diet. Preferring to work the ground, it needs no leaf or limb pattern on its pelage. The plain coat may be either a deep shade of gray or russet. Animals of different colors interbreed. Young of both colors may appear in a litter.

The jaguarundi is one of the least known cats on the continent, its life history and population not yet well documented. And now may be too late. Already a rare animal, it becomes even rarer as its habitat—wild thickets and dense

lowland forest—is sheared and put to ranching and farm use.

Mating time for this "otter cat" seems to vary with the locality. The litter of two or three kittens is born after a gestation period known from captive animals to be 72 to 75 days. As in most other cats, kits in the wild probably are cared for solely by their mother.

Full grown, the jaguarundi stands up to 14 inches (36 cm) at the shoulder. Its tail accounts for nearly half its length of 35 to 55 inches (89 to 140 cm). A large individual may weigh as much as 20 pounds (9 kg).

Jaguar (*Panthera onca*)

A favorite hangout of the jaguar is out on a limb dangling over a stream in a sultry southern forest. *P. onca* is very fond of fish. Indians in Brazil believe it flicks the surface of the water with the tip of its tail to lure fish within reach of its claws. It swims expertly, sometimes pursuing the South American caiman in tropical streams. Deer, along with capybaras, tapirs, peccaries, and other small mammals probably are more frequent prey. In ranch country it may also eat livestock.

The jaguar stalks its prey or ambushes it from a hiding place.

Largest of all the New World cats, the jaguar is heavier than its Old World relative, the leopard, and has a more massive chest. Adults vary from 5 to 8 feet (152 to 244 cm) in total length and 100 to 250 pounds (45 to 113 kg) in weight.

The jaguar's short, stiff coat is golden or cinnamon buff, spotted with black rosettes. Melanistic individuals with dark brown or black coats are not uncommon.

Jaguars once ranged southern California and eastern Texas, and north as far as the Grand Canyon.

The last one recorded in California was killed at Palm Springs about 1860. Any resident populations in the United States were eliminated by the early 1900's. Individuals, however, continued to wander up from Mexico. The most recent records are from southern Texas in 1948 and southeastern Arizona in 1949 and 1971.

In Mexico the jaguar lives in low coastal forests, north along the Gulf Coast to the mouth of the Rio Grande, and on the Pacific side to the Sonoran foothills of the Sierra Madre. From Mexico it ranges southward to Argentina.

The jaguar, known as *el tigre* in Spanish, has a coughing roar of five or six loud guttural notes.

The gestation period is about 100 days. Two to four young are born in a cave or other sheltered spot.

The jaguar has been relentlessly hunted as a livestock killer and for its valuable coat. In a 1972 survey, Dr. Carl Koford estimated that there were fewer than 1,000 jaguars left in all Mexico and fewer than 100 in Argentina.

Lynx (*Felis lynx*)

Feast tonight, fast tomorrow. So goes the hunting pattern of the Canada lynx. Stealthily creeping on big cat feet, spreading its toes where the snow lies soft, the lynx must stalk undetected to within a few bounds of the snowshoe hare or the quarry may escape. Hunter and hunted are well matched. Both are creatures of boreal forest, and so closely is lynx economy linked to the hare that populations of prey and predator peak and crash—almost in unison—once a decade. When a hare depression hits an area,

lynxes move en masse, some of them even entering large cities. Though breeding takes place as usual, in late winter, and kittens—one to four—are born 60 to 65 days after mating, few kittens survive in a season of famine.

When times improve, populations begin to rebuild. Born looking and sounding much like the litter of a house cat—but larger and louder—lynx kittens are fed, protected, and taught feline survival ways by the female with no aid from the wild tom. In captivity, however, males have shown paternal solicitude, playing with and grooming kittens.

An old, well-fed male of this north country species may weigh up to 40 pounds (18 kg). To a head and body length of 32 to 36 inches (81 to 91 cm) a stubby tail adds a mere 4 inches (10.2 cm). Females are slightly smaller than males. Larger ear tufts, longer sideburns, and a black-tipped tail distinguish the lynx from its close kin, the bobcat. The long, soft grayish-buff fur of the lynx is lightly mottled with brown. This luxurious fur has made the lynx a target of trappers for 300 years.

Bobcat (*Felis rufus*)

The stub that earns *F. rufus* its common name is not much. It is too short to be of real use in balancing its owner—which is 28 to 49 inches (71 to 124 cm) long. But the bobcat does manage to climb, scramble, and pounce without rudder-assist. Why a tail at all? Picture a female bobcat out hunting, her three-month-old kittens tagging along in the dense underbrush. The mother holds her tail curved up. Its tip is black only on the upper side. From behind, the white underside is clearly visible, serving as a "follow me" signal to the kittens.

A young bobcat at about seven months old advances a stage in its apprenticeship. It begins to spend time hunting alone on its mother's home range, then returning, perhaps because the hunt has not gone well and it wants the consolation of a full stomach before soloing again. The young become independent at 9 to 12 months and then leave the area where they were reared to search for their own territories.

Adult bobcats lead solitary lives except at breeding time, usually

late winter to spring. A male's home range may overlap those of a few females, but they normally avoid encounters by using different parts of the area. During short periods of severe winter weather, neighboring adults may waive the rules and share the same rock-pile shelter, neither threatening nor socializing with one another.

The bobcat, more adaptable to disturbed habitats, has the widest distribution of all Nearctic cats. But its numbers have plummeted in recent years due to heavy trapping.

The high, shady limb of a live oak
gives a captive bobcat a vantage
point and relief from the heat of
day. Reclusive by nature, a bobcat
at bay may hiss, spit, and snarl—
and stand off many times its weight
in dogs or barehanded humans.
The mother and kitten opposite
put to use the superb sensory
equipment of nighttime hunters:
keen eyesight, sensitive whiskers,
and tufts of hair on the ears that
act as antennae to aid hearing.

Though well-equipped to find food,
cats and other carnivores rarely
kill above their needs. Some can
live in relative harmony close to
people. For others, wilderness
areas afford more congenial habitats.

Seals, Sea Lions & Walruses

Order Pinnipedia

A walrus, its hide wrinkled and marked with many tubercles, casts a wary eye toward a photographer in Bristol Bay, Alaska. A bristly moustache helps the huge pinniped feel its way to buried clams.

"Northern Fur Seal Studies" was the subject of my talk to a businessmen's luncheon group. When I had finished and asked for questions, a hand went up in the middle of the room: "Could you explain by what means seals are able to breathe water?" This question so astonished me that from that time on I have started my talks on seals by saying: "Seals are air-breathing, warm-blooded, milk-producing, hair-covered aquatic descendants of land mammals that returned to the sea some 25 million years ago."

At that time an ancestor of present-day otters took to the ancient sea. About eight million years later an early representative of present-day bears also became aquatic. All "seals" trace their ancestry back to these.

The order Pinnipedia (meaning "fin-footed") contains three modern families. The members of two of them are commonly called seals, and those of the third, walruses. The Phocidae, or "earless" seals (also called true seals), are believed to be descendants of the early otter; the Otariidae, or "eared" seals, of the early bear. Walruses are probably most closely related to the eared seals.

Because the marine environment differs drastically from our terrestrial environment, all marine mammals have evolved special adaptations. Powerfully equipped with webbed, five-toed hind limbs and streamlined foreflippers, pinnipeds dive expertly. But earless seals, whose ancestors returned to the sea first, go deeper and stay down longer than eared seals. Instruments recorded a Weddell seal descending 1,800 feet and remaining submerged for almost an hour. By contrast, a California sea lion's deepest dive fell 1,000 feet short of that; and a northern fur seal's longest dive lasted less than six minutes.

Physiological adaptations slow down heartbeat and metabolism and conserve oxygen stored in the blood while diving. To maintain relatively high body temperature in often frigid environments, pinnipeds have developed blubber—fatty tissue under the skin that encases almost the entire body.

Fur seals have such a dense coat of fine fur that water never penetrates to the skin. Fur soiled by oil, however, loses its water-repellent characteristics, and I suspect that seals affected by an oil spill become chilled and die. Even on land, pinnipeds are often exposed to a chilly environment. I found such a place on a springtime visit to San Miguel Island, off California.

The wind, thick with fog, swirled up over a low bluff that bordered a hundred yards of sand beach, and the air was heavy with sounds and smells. Barely visible through the mist, a colony of California sea lions was beginning the spring pupping season. Bleating pups, hungry to nurse, searched for mothers. Sleek and dripping, females returning from the sea called repeatedly to their young. Above this bedlam adult males barked as they guarded bits of territory. In the foreground, between me and the sea lion colony, northern elephant seals crowded the beach—seals and sea lions sharing different parts of the same rookery. The elephant seals were mostly weaned pups that had been born in midwinter.

During my visits I have observed differences between the phocid elephant seals and the otariid sea lions on the San Miguel beach. A bull elephant seal, emerging from the water, lay prone. Then, like a giant maggot, he hitched his 5,000-pound body up the beach. His great hulk seemed to flow over the sand on rhythmic waves of blubber, with only a minimum of help from the foreflippers. Elephant seals cannot rotate their hind flippers to move forward. But sea lions can. Progressing on hind legs that extend only from the

Flipping sand over his back, a young male elephant seal protects himself from rays of the sun. As a species, the northern elephant seal gets another kind of protection: laws that prohibit hunting.

ankles down, sea lions waddle with a rolling gait, as clumsy as children in a sack race.

Although they exhibit obvious differences, the phocid and otariid seals have much in common. They all eat other marine animals, sharing the characteristic of meat-eating with carnivores descended from related ancestors. Walruses glide along the sea bottom sucking up clams. Interestingly, they discard the shells, and only the undamaged clam meats are found in their stomachs. Rinsed in seawater, the meats are a prized delicacy to Eskimos. I must admit I enjoyed my share of these clams after hunters shot a walrus near Little Diomede Island, Alaska.

Fur seals, sea lions, and harbor seals often come into conflict with fishermen south of the Bering Sea ice pack. Each spring, Steller's sea lions gather by the thousands on Aleutian Islands adjacent to the waters of Unimak Pass, where salmon migrate toward spawning streams that empty into Bristol Bay. Fishermen assume the sea lions are

there for the salmon, but the evidence is lacking. Sea lion stomachs I have examined contained octopus and small bottom fishes.

Many pinniped species are innately tame. This is surely the result of the seals' evolution in an environment free of dangerous predators, at least when on land. Such species as the Alaska fur seal and the monk seals, which inhabit remote oceanic islands, seem unable to overcome their lack of fear in the interest of self-preservation.

Every summer, Alaska fur seals are driven from their hauling grounds to killing fields. Certain individuals which, for one reason or another (such as a scarred pelt), are allowed to escape, return day after day and even year after year. They make the trip from the hauling ground to the killing field repeatedly, seemingly unable to learn they should flee.

Monk seals appear to be extreme in their inability to withstand human intrusion. The Caribbean species was the first large mammal discovered by Columbus on his second

voyage in 1493. As western people occupied the islands of the Caribbean, the seals gradually disappeared. Having been isolated for millions of years on tropical or subtropical islets, they had not developed the ability to flee and were easily clubbed by anyone who landed on their basking and pupping beaches. As a result, the Caribbean monk seal may be extinct. The last reliable sighting was in 1952.

In 1973 the U. S. Fish and Wildlife Service sent me on an extensive aerial survey of all areas where this seal had been recorded in the last century. The most notable observation we made was that on every island we surveyed we saw signs of human intrusion.

Only two other species of monk seals exist today, the Hawaiian and the Mediterranean. Whether these two relict species can long survive is difficult to predict. Although they appear to be naturally tame, they seem incapable of tolerating human presence when mothers are nursing pups.

A burly northern fur seal bull mates with a sleek female hardly a quarter his size on a beach in the Pribilof Islands. When cows come ashore in the spring, the breeding male gathers a harem on his section of defended beach.

For example, Hawaii's westernmost island, Kure, was not occupied by people until 1960, when a U. S. Coast Guard station was established there. Counts in 1957 and 1958 had indicated that the population of monk seals on Kure was at least 150 animals. Twenty years later only 50 seals remained, all but two of them adults. It was observed that soon after weaning—by abandonment, as is normal—many pups disappeared. To understand why, remember that before people came to Kure most baby seals were born on high, shrub-bordered beaches surrounded by shallow water. After humans occupied the island, however, monk seal mothers moved to isolated sand spits to bear their young. These shifting, storm-swept islets were near deep water prowled by sharks that doubtless found the pups easy prey. As a result, the Kure population may be doomed to the Caribbean monk seal's fate.

Its near relative, the elephant seal, faced extinction early this century. Sealers had systematically slaughtered entire colonies on islands off the California coast. Fewer than 100 sea elephants survived, the nucleus of today's teeming thousands on Guadalupe Island. At Año Nuevo Reserve, on the California mainland just north of Santa Cruz, visitors may approach to within 25 feet of breeding and basking elephant seals. Their ability to tolerate people has apparently enabled them to regain high population levels.

Today many colonies of seals, protected by laws against exploitation, are returning to ancestral breeding grounds. In some areas controlled harvesting of certain pinnipeds—the northern fur seal, for example—may prove beneficial to the survival of a species.

But in the Bering Sea a sinister new danger looms—fishermen's discarded nets. Made of long-lasting synthetics, they float like kelp, tempting curious fur seals. Many become ensnared and starve to death.

Pinnipeds are highly adapted denizens of the harshest environments inhabited by mammals. One of the most unusual adaptations is the ability to fast for prolonged periods. When the mother Hawaiian monk seal comes ashore to bear her pup, she is enormously fat. In her three-inch blubber layer there is enough nutritive value to sustain both herself and her pup for six weeks. During that time she will not leave her pup to find food for herself.

Her pup will quadruple its 35-pound birth weight by the time the mother abruptly weans it. She is gaunt, having lost two pounds for each one gained by her pup.

Among eared seals, males fast during the breeding season. To protect his harem from other males, a bull fur seal must remain on his territory. One that I marked with yellow paint held vigil for 64 days without going to sea to find food for himself.

Pinnipeds are marvelously resilient too. When a conservation consciousness began to flourish in the early 20th century, the animals responded. By the mid-1950's all North American pinniped species, except the monk seal and the Guadalupe fur seal, were no longer endangered. By 1970, many—the Pacific walrus, northern fur seal, California and Steller's sea lions, and harbor seals, for example—were at or approaching the maximum populations their habitats could support.

Many wildlife protectionists urge us not to exercise population management in any exploitive sense, but to extend complete protection to all pinniped species. On the other hand, a growing human appetite for fishery products—in areas where seals compete with human needs—leads others to urge control of pinnipeds. These people contend that where large pinniped populations interfere with human efforts to obtain maximum yields from ocean fisheries, the seal numbers should be kept within certain limits.

Regardless of what management, conservation, and protective policies are undertaken, it appears certain that the vast majority of pinniped populations are in no immediate danger of excessive exploitation. But environmental pollution by oil, radioactive wastes, and, indeed, discarded fish nets pose future threats to pinnipeds.   KARL W. KENYON

An adolescent Hawaiian monk seal swims between submerged coral heads in the Leeward Islands, which have long been protected as part of the Hawaiian Islands National Wildlife Refuge. Found only in the Leewards, this monk seal was first studied extensively in 1957. Surveys made then indicated that the population of this endangered species exceeded 1,200. But surveys conducted in 1977 and 1978 indicate that the overall population has since decreased by about 50 percent.

Family Otariidae

Seal watchers see members of this family
from the Alaskan Arctic to Baja California.
A pointed snout breaks the surface just
offshore. Or a pod of seals basks
in the sun and surf (right) of Oregon's
rocky coast. They belong to the family
of eared seals: 13 species, four of which
can be seen in the coastal waters of
North America. Other species breed on
many sub-Antarctic islands in the South
Atlantic, South Pacific, and Indian Oceans.
All stemmed from bearlike carnivores
that lived some 17 million years ago.

The eared seals are divided into two
subfamilies: the Arctocephalinae, or fur
seals, with eight species; and the Otariinae,
or sea lions, with five species. Fur seals
have a more pointed snout than sea lions
have. They also have a thick layer of
underfur beneath a sparse outer coat of stiff
guard hairs. Sea lions have no undercoat.

All members of the family have small
external ears and closely set teeth that are
sharp and conical—ideal for seizing fish,
squid, octopus, and other prey. Their hind
limbs can be rotated forward for getting
about on land. The fore and hind flippers
have bare black palms and cartilaginous
extensions beyond the tips of the digits.
The fingers of the oarlike foreflippers
decrease in size from the first to the
fifth; all fingers have rudimentary nails.

Many members of this family—and of
the other pinniped families as well—exhibit
the phenomenon of delayed implantation.
After the female has mated, her fertilized
egg goes through preliminary stages
of development but then ceases all growth
for some weeks or months before
becoming attached to the uterine wall
and resuming development.

Northern Fur Seal (*Callorhinus ursinus*)

For nearly 200 years the northern fur seal has been exploited for its thick and velvety undercoat— averaging some 300,000 fine hairs per square inch. Today it is one of the world's most carefully managed wild species.

During winter, fur seals range through open seas from Japan to the Bering Sea, southward as far as Baja California. With spring's coming, however, they begin to congregate on their far northern breeding grounds. Some 450,000 of them travel to traditional rookeries on the Commander, Kuril, and Robben islands, all owned by the Soviet Union. The greatest population—some 1,300,000—head for the Pribilof Islands' age-old breeding beaches.

First to arrive in May are the big, breeding males, at least 10 years old, and ranging from 6 to 7 feet (1.8 to 2.1 m) in length and weighing about 600 pounds (272 kg). Each bull stakes

out a breeding territory (as the male above has done) and defends it against all rivals. Younger males, unable to compete with their elders, haul out on separate bachelor beaches.

The much smaller females, up to 5 feet (1.5 m) in length and weighing 130 pounds (59 kg), reach the Pribilofs by late June.

Within two days of her arrival, each cow gives birth to a black-furred pup. Several days later, the female mates with a bull, whose harem may number 40 or 50.

The mother seal alternates periods of nursing her pup with week-long hunting trips at sea. On her return, she unerringly locates her own pup among thousands of others by its distinctive smell and call. The youngster may double its weight by fall, when its mother leaves the pup to fend for itself.

When the United States acquired Alaska and the Pribilofs from Russia in 1867, the seal colonies were large and thriving. But by 1910 hunters had reduced the herds from some 2,500,000 to about 200,000. Today kills are regulated, with about 28,000 bachelor seals harvested annually.

Guadalupe Fur Seal (*Arctocephalus townsendi*)

Once abundant along the California coast, from the Farallon and Channel islands to Mexico's Guadalupe Island, this seal was almost wiped out by hunters in the early 19th century. But a remnant survived until 1894 when the species virtually disappeared. Many zoologists considered it extinct.

In 1928, however, two fishermen discovered about 60 of the seals on Guadalupe. They captured two and sold them to the San Diego Zoo. In a dispute over payment, one fisherman reputedly threatened to exterminate all the rest. He may have almost succeeded, for there was no record of any Guadalupe fur seal for the next 21 years. Once again it was considered extinct.

Then, in 1949, one lone male was sighted on San Nicolas Island off southern California, and five years later a breeding colony of 14 was discovered on the seal's namesake island. Under protection, the group has increased to about 1,000. The main threat today—except for such natural enemies as sharks and killer whales—seems to be disturbances from tour boats that visit the islands regularly during the breeding season.

One of two species of fur seal in North American waters, the Guadalupe differs from the northern fur seal by having a longer, more pointed snout. Its fur extends beyond the wrist and into the foreflipper's upper surface.

The bull measures about 6 feet (1.8 m) long and weighs 300 pounds (136 kg). Females are considerably larger than northern fur seal cows.

Northern Sea Lion (*Eumetopias jubata*)

You can usually see them on Seal Rocks, near San Francisco's Golden Gate Bridge, and around the Sea Lion Caves on the Oregon coast. They are northern sea lions—also known as Steller's sea lions. That name recalls the man who first studied and described them. Georg Wilhelm Steller was the naturalist with a Russian expedition, led by Vitus Bering, that explored the approaches to Alaska in 1741.

Largest of all the eared seals, northern sea lion bulls range to 13 feet (4 m) in length and may weigh as much as 2,400 pounds (1,089 kg). The females are about 7 feet (2.1 m) long, and weigh 700 pounds (318 kg). These sea lions have a coat of short, coarse hair with almost no underfur. Deep-voiced, the big bulls bellow with a throaty roar. Pups bleat like lambs.

An inhabitant of coastal waters and offshore islands, the northern sea lion ranges through the North Pacific from the coasts of Japan and Kamchatka to the islands of the Bering Sea and coastal Alaska, and southward to California's Channel Islands. World population is estimated at 250,000 or more, with about 200,000 in Alaskan rookeries, mostly in the Aleutians.

Bulls don't eat in the breeding season. They establish territories in early May and collect harems of 10 to 30 cows, guarding them (as the bull does above) until the breeding season ends. Bulls then usually leave to travel northward.

The 40-pound (18-kg) pup is born in late May or early June, and the females mate within a few days after giving birth. Sometimes the youngster nurses for nearly a year.

Northern sea lions eat octopus, squid, crab, and a great variety of fishes, diving as deep as 600 feet after prey. Fishermen dislike them—and California sea lions—because they sometimes eat commercial fish and damage nets and other gear. For many years Canada has worked to control the numbers of northern sea lions in its waters. In a single year hunters in British Columbia killed about 8,000, cutting the provincial population from 12,000 to about 4,000.

California Sea Lion (*Zalophus californianus*)

Adaptable and highly intelligent, this is the familiar performing seal that entertains at circuses and zoos the world over.

Smaller than its northern kin, the adult male measures about 8 feet (2.4 m) in length and weighs 600 pounds (272 kg). A bony crest crowns the male. (The one above barks—never a roar—in Monterey Bay, California, a favorite hauling ground and tourist-boat site.) A female seldom measures more than 6 feet (1.8 m) and weighs a third as much as her mate.

The California sea lion inhabits coastal waters from the Farallons near San Francisco to the Tres Marias Islands off Mexico. The population is about 80,000, divided between the waters of Mexico and the United States.

A swift and graceful swimmer, this sea lion, like all the eared seals, propels itself with its broad front flippers, and steers with its rear flippers. It is a gregarious and playful animal that sometimes rolls over and over, then pops out of the water like a cork and onto a rocky shore.

Bulls establish territories in the summer breeding season, but females move freely from one area to another. A 12- to 14-pound (5.4- to 6.4-kg) pup is usually born in June. After the breeding season, adult and subadult males often move northward, as far as British Columbia.

A young California sea lion shows 10-mph form swimming in the Gulf of California.

Family Odobenidae

The walrus is the only pinniped whose upper canine teeth have evolved into long, downward-thrusting tusks. A moustache of about 400 stiff but sensitive bristles adorns its broad muzzle. The body is thick and heavy—a large adult male weighed 3,432 pounds (1,557 kg)—and the wrinkled, almost naked skin of adult males is marked by many lumps and tubercles. Females and young are covered by short, rust-brown hair. A fold of skin encloses the tail.

Closely allied to the eared seals, the walrus stemmed from ancestral members of that group some 15 million years ago. Like eared seals, it can rotate its hind limbs forward, and so it can walk on land. Like earless seals, it has no external ear cartilage; each ear opening is protected by a flap of skin.

Walruses mostly eat clams gathered from the sea floor. A walrus sometimes dives 300 feet when feeding, and it may remain below for up to 10 minutes. A common belief is that a walrus uses its tusks to pry clams loose from the bottom. Zoologists say the muzzle and bristles alone root up the food. Then lips and tongue suck the soft flesh from the shells.

Pacific Walrus (*Odobenus rosmarus divergens*)

After spending the summer months feeding in the Chukchi Sea, herds of Pacific walruses move southward in the fall ahead of the ice pack, passing through Bering Strait and spending the winter in the Bering Sea. When spring comes, the movement is reversed. Walruses breed on the ice floes in February and March, and most males bear scars of battles for mates. (The bull above rests between rounds.)

Groups of adult bulls—each may weigh about 3,000 pounds (1,361 kg)—are usually the first to head through the straits. Next come adult females with their newborn calves and immature

young. Walrus cows bear only one calf every other year. About 4 feet (1.2 m) long and weighing from 85 to 160 pounds (39 to 73 kg) at birth, the Pacific walrus young nurses for nearly two years. If a calf gets tired while swimming beside its mother, it may hitch a ride on her neck or back. When she dives to the bottom for a meal of shellfish, she sometimes grasps the calf in her flippers and carries it along.

A few walruses become "rogues," eating carrion, or attacking and killing seals and other prey for food. One rogue walrus was seen feeding on a freshly killed narwhal some 14 feet long.

Siberian and Alaskan natives have traditionally used walrus hides for their boats, walrus flesh for both human and dog food, blubber for oil, sinews for cordage, tusks for tools and ivory carvings.

The ATLANTIC WALRUS (*Odobenus rosmarus rosmarus*), slightly smaller than its Pacific cousin, is found from the Kara Sea westward to the Canadian Arctic, and southward to Labrador and Hudson Bay. Once it ranged as far south as the Gulf of St. Lawrence, occasionally to Cape Cod.

Wrinkled hide up to two inches thick serves as effective armor when walruses spar (above). Tusks sometimes exceed two feet in length. They are used as weapons against killer whales and polar bears. Hooked into the edge of an ice cake, tusks help a walrus lever its heavy body out of the water. The animal's scientific name means "tooth-walking sea-horse."

A walrus often uses its tusks to prod a neighbor, signaling it to move over and make room when the animals huddle close on the beach (opposite). If danger threatens, an alert animal bellows to rouse the sleeping herd.

Walruses lying together share warmth. After a prolonged dive in frigid waters, the skin becomes pale (right), for the animal's blood has been concentrated deep within its body. After lying in the arctic sunshine for awhile, the walrus regains its color.

Family Phocidae

Sleek in the sea, ungainly on land, members
of this family live all over the world,
usually in coastal waters. Five species
inhabit antarctic or far southern seas and
eight live in arctic or northern temperate
waters. Monk seals range through
tropical seas. And two other species—the
Baikal and Caspian seals—live in inland
waters that are, respectively, fresh and salt.
All swim sinuously, moving a streamlined
body in somewhat the same way a fish
propels itself through the water.

On land, all members of the family move
laboriously, with a humping, caterpillarlike
locomotion, their hind flippers dragging.
Unlike walruses and eared seals, phocids
cannot rotate their hind flippers forward.
The furred foreflippers help steer and
brake. Adult coats are of short, stiff hair
with little undercoat. Young of many
species are born with white, woolly coats.

These seals all stem from otterlike
carnivores that lived some 25 million years
ago. They range in size from the giant
southern elephant seal, which is 20 feet
(6 m) long, to the little ringed seal, whose
average length is less than 5 feet (1.5 m).

Like walruses, phocids have no external
ears. That is why the 17 living species in
this family are called the earless seals.

Harbor Seal (*Phoca vitulina*)

A smooth round head with dark,
bulging eyes rises from the water,
then quickly submerges. Flipping
over on its back, the harbor seal
swims upside down just beneath
the surface, sculling with its
hind flippers. Near shore, it
turns right side up and humps
its way onto the beach.

The harbor seal—also known as
the common or hair seal—averages
5 feet (1.5 m) in length and weighs
200 pounds (91 kg) as an adult.
Its short-haired coat varies from
cream to brownish black in
background color, interrupted by
countless blotches and spots.

Widest ranging of all seals, the harbor seal inhabits coastal waters throughout much of the Northern Hemisphere. In the Atlantic it is found from the Arctic and coasts of northern Europe southward to France and Georgia. In the North Pacific it ranges from the Bering and Okhotsk seas southward as far as Japan and Korea in Asiatic waters, and Baja California on the western coast of North America. One landlocked form of the species is found in Canada's Seal Lakes, east of Hudson Bay.

Harbor seals hunt octopus, squid, and other small marine animals, sometimes diving as deep as 300 feet and remaining underwater for more than 20 minutes. They also dine on salmon or other commercial fishes, and many fishermen do not like them. Canada has had a bounty on them for years, but they are protected in U. S. waters.

Males establish no territories and gather no harems. Mating takes place in the water. Pups, covered with a blue-gray coat, usually are born in May or June on a beach. The pup can swim immediately. Sometimes it must; the next high tide may submerge its birthplace.

Ribbon Seal (*Phoca fasciata*)

This handsome species, also called the banded seal, gets its common name from the distinctive coat of the male (above): a background of deep, chocolate brown, interrupted by broad, creamy-white stripes that encircle the neck, front flippers, and the rump. The female is much paler and grayer than her mate. Adults of both sexes average about 5 feet (1.5 m) in length, and 200 pounds (91 kg) in weight.

Rarest of all northern seals, the species occurs in two distinct populations: one group of about 100,000 in the Bering-Chukchi Sea area; the other—perhaps 130,000 seals—farther westward in the Sea of Okhotsk. There does not seem to be any intermingling of the two.

The Bering-Chukchi population spends the winter and spring along the southern edge of the pack ice, and the white-coated pups are born on sea ice in March or April after a 9½-month gestation period.

Russian traders once used the banded coats as coverings for trunks. Eskimos made clothes bags of the skins. As related by mammalogist E. W. Nelson, "The skin is removed entire and then tanned, the only opening left being a long slit in the abdomen, which is provided with eyelet holes and a lacing string, thus making a convenient water-proof bag...."

Ringed Seal (*Phoca hispida*)

Most abundant of all the arctic seals, the ringed seal numbers in the millions but is essentially solitary. Circumpolar, it ranges ice-bound arctic coasts. In the Bering and Chukchi seas, ringed seals move north and south each year with the pack ice. In the Canadian Arctic, they stay in the same general area all year.

The color of their coats varies from gray to blue-black with many creamy, dark-centered rings. Adults of both sexes average only 4.5 feet (1.4 m) in length and weigh about 200 pounds (91 kg). They are the smallest of all pinnipeds.

When the sea freezes over, the seal makes breathing holes in the ice, using teeth and claws to keep them open. A polar bear hunting for food sometimes kills a seal emerging to breathe.

A pregnant seal digs out or adapts a snow den on landlocked ice (below), and there has her pup. She comes and goes unseen through a hole in the floor. But a polar bear may find the den, smash it in, and seize the pup.

The pup is born, white-coated, between mid-March and early May. It will nurse for nearly two months before its mother leaves it.

Harp Seal (*Pagophilus groenlandicus*)

"The ice lover from Greenland," as its scientific name translates, spends the summer near that great northern island, feeding among ice floes of the Greenland Sea and Canada's eastern arctic.

The population splits in the fall, one part heading for the White Sea, where females bear their pups in late winter, then breed. Another group travels to an area north of Jan Mayen Island and does the same. Members of the third and by far the largest group drift southward with the ice floes until they reach their breeding grounds in the Gulf of St. Lawrence and on "the front"—the ice fields east of Labrador and Newfoundland. There pregnant females haul out on the ice to bear their pups.

Adults of both sexes are about the same size: 6 feet (1.8 m) in length, 300 to 400 pounds (136 to 181 kg) in weight. The male is silvery gray, with a black head and a horseshoe-shaped band from shoulder to flank. This bold marking gives the species its common names: harp or saddleback seal.

Markings of the female (above, with newborn pup) are usually paler.

The newborn pup weighs about 12 pounds (5.4 kg) and has fluffy white fur that gives it the name "whitecoat." It nurses for 10 to 14 days, increasing its weight fivefold or more—mostly blubber— by the time it is weaned and abandoned. The pup lives off its fat and moults its white coat for a smooth coat of gray hairs.

Seal hunters prize the pelt, which they must take before the moult begins. Because of heavy hunting over the years, Canada's breeding population, once totaling 2,500,000 or more, is now less than 1,000,000. Despite outcry against the Canadian hunt, the killing goes on as usual every winter. And, in spite of the species' reduced population, the Canadian government has increased the kill quota of harp seal pups in recent years.

Gray Seal (*Halichoerus grypus*)

Every summer a hundred or more gray seals appear in Maine waters, hauling out to sun themselves on the approaches to Mount Desert Island and the islands of Penobscot Bay. Some 200 miles to the south, a band of 15 or 20 live year-round on shoal islands in Nantucket Sound. There their pups are born in January or February in the ice off Muskeget Island. These are the southernmost breeders of all the gray seals in the western North Atlantic.

Gray seals have three distinct centers of population: the waters of southeastern Canada; northern Europe from the British Isles to the White Sea; and the Baltic Sea.

The total population of 50,000 or more may be increasing in many areas. Canada's gray seals, numbering 5,000—and possibly several times that—seem to be thriving. Nearly 2,000 pups were counted on Nova Scotia's Sable Island in a recent year.

Males and females differ in size (as the two above show). A big bull may measure 9.8 feet (3 m), and weigh 640 pounds (290 kg). Females usually measure some 7.6 feet (2.3 m) and weigh 550 pounds (249 kg). The bull's coat ranges from dark gray to almost black, with many spots and markings. The female's lighter background has dark spots. A prominent nose gives the species another name: horsehead seal.

Unlike most seals, bulls are territorial, gathering harems of pregnant females. A pup weighs 30 pounds (14 kg) at birth and may triple that weight when it is weaned at about three weeks of age.

Many fishermen look upon the gray seal as a thieving nuisance, and for a number of years the Maritime Provinces of Canada have offered a bounty on the species. Nova Scotia conducts an annual "cull" of the seals by commercial hunters working under the supervision of fisheries officers.

Hooded Seal (*Cystophora cristata*)

A unique bit of anatomy, the male seal's nasal pouch, gives this species its common names: hooded, crested, or bladdernose seal. The pouch, also called a hood, usually hangs limp and wrinkled over his nose. But it can be inflated to twice the size of a soccer ball. Experts debate why the male swells his pouch. It may be excitement. (Or anger, which the male at right may be showing a photographer.) An inflatable nasal membrane—it looks like a bright red balloon— can also be pushed out of a nostril.

An adult male averages 6.5 to 10 feet (2 to 3 m) and weighs 700 to 900 pounds (318 to 408 kg). His hair is bluish or gray, marked with darker spots and blotches. The female (in foreground above, with pup) is smaller and paler than her mate and lacks a nasal hood.

Most of the world's 500,000 hooded seals live in the East Greenland Sea and breed north of Iceland and Jan Mayen Island. Between 50,000 and 75,000 breed in the pack ice off Labrador, Newfoundland, and the Gulf of St. Lawrence.

Hunters kill as many as 15,000 hooded seals each year in Canadian waters during breeding season.

Northern Elephant Seal (*Mirounga angustirostris*)

The elephant seals, largest of all seals, get their common name from the trunklike proboscis dangling from the muzzle of adult males. The snout is an extension of the nasal cavities and, when inflated, curves into the seal's mouth. This acts as a resonating chamber in the throat when the bull snorts or bellows. This elephant seal and its Southern Hemisphere kin, *M. leonina*, are anatomically similar.

The northern species once inhabited breeding rookeries and hauling grounds on offshore islands from Baja California to the Farallons. In the 19th century they were ruthlessly hunted, for a large bull—an easy victim—could yield up to 200 gallons of fine oil. The species was almost extinct by 1890; fewer than 100 survived at Guadalupe Island, Mexico. Then, in 1922, the Mexican Government began protecting them. They steadily increased, and today they number 50,000 or more.

Adult bulls come ashore on the breeding beaches in November and December, fighting one another as they establish territories. Karl Kenyon describes an encounter: "An established bull rose up to offer a bellowing challenge to the intruder, and the two aggressive beasts faced each other chest to chest before separating to rest while eyeing one another on either side of an invisible but well-established territorial boundary."

Males may measure 17 feet (5 m) and weigh 5,000 pounds (2,268 kg). Cows range to 11 feet (3.4 m) and 2,000 pounds (907 kg).

Pregnant cows arrive at the hauling-out grounds in December; within a few days each gives birth to a dark-haired pup. (An angry mother guards the one above.) By the time the pup is weaned—at about four weeks—it has tripled or quadrupled its birth weight.

Dueling for dominance, bulls bleed but rarely die. The fight may be a one-minute round, ending when the vanquished gives ground.

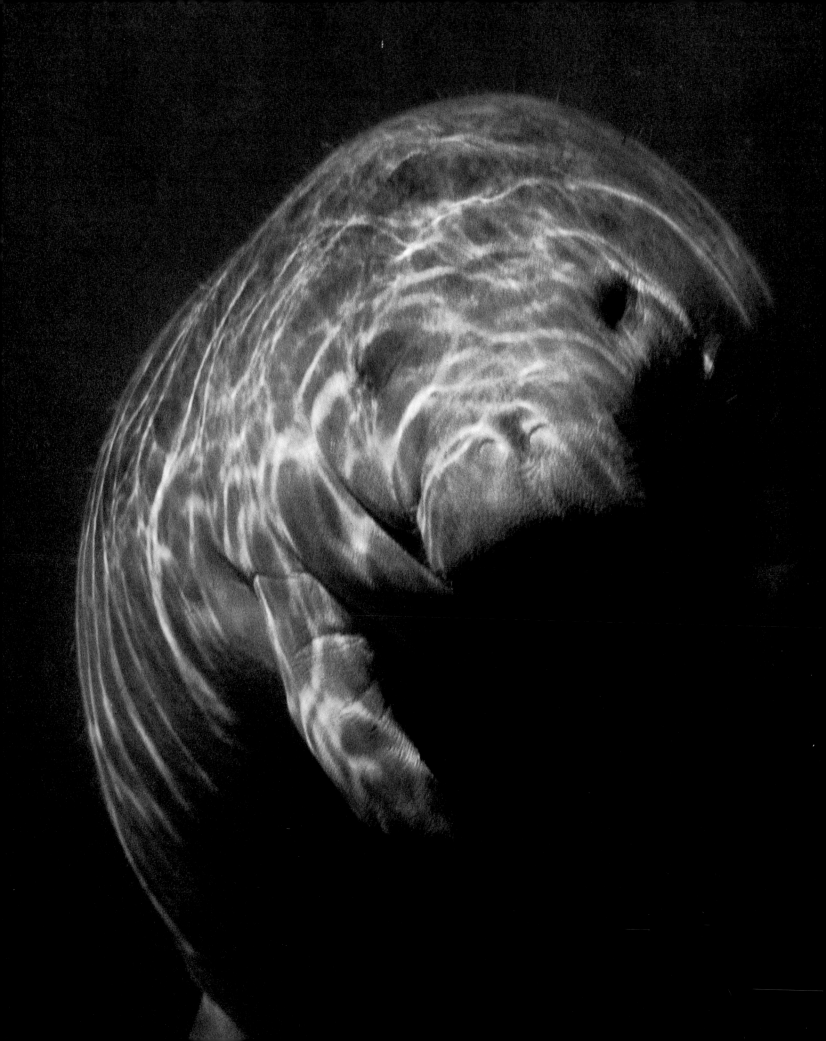

The Manatee

Order Sirenia

A Florida manatee, member of a species that nears extinction, sets a course through waters as murky as its future. Many bear the scars of civilization—gashes made by propellers of speeding boats.

Homely and ungainly, without the grace of dolphins or the grandeur of whales, the sea cow seems an unlikely inspiration for ancient tales of alluring mermaids. But presumably the animal did inspire such stories, and it remained for explorers of the New World to explode the myth. Grumped one 16th-century Spanish chronicler, "So ugly is [the manatee], that uglier it cannot get."

Today only four sea cow species survive, most of them living in shallow tropical marine waters and the larger tropical rivers of the world. A fifth species, Steller's sea cow, *Hydrodamalis stelleri,* roamed the frigid Bering Sea until fur and seal hunters exterminated it around 1769—fewer than 30 years after it was first reported.

Three of the still-surviving species are called manatees. They belong to the family Trichechidae. The fourth is the dugong, of the family Dugongidae. And all are called sirenians—in memory of their mythic beauty.

Only one species, the West Indian manatee, *Trichechus manatus,* frequents the waters of the continental United States. It ranges northward along Florida's Gulf and Atlantic coasts—occasionally as far as the Carolinas—and south to below the Amazon River. (Another species, *T. inunguis,* confines itself to the Amazon River and its tributaries, and an African species, *T. senegalensis,* ranges the coastal waters and larger rivers from Senegal to Angola.)

Sirenians are large, seal-shaped animals with front flippers and a horizontally flattened tail. They are warm-blooded and breathe air. Adults vary in size from about eight to twelve feet and weigh from several hundred to more than a thousand pounds. (The extinct Steller's sea cow, a giant among sirenians, attained a length of 20 feet or more.) The thick, tough skin of sirenians is only sparsely haired, except for numerous stout bristles on the face.

Sea cows probably share a common ancestry with elephants, whose fossil remains date back some 50 million years. Sirenians' molars, like those of elephants, are continuously replaced with new teeth that move forward from the back of the jaw as the old ones wear down and are pushed out.

These animals are unique among mammals in that they are the only herbivores to spend their entire lives in the water. And they are gentle. A sea cow will not fight—even to save its own life. When faced with danger, its only defense is a hasty retreat at speeds of up to 20 miles an hour.

Sirenians spend much of their time grazing on submerged beds of sea grass and other aquatic vegetation. Several animals may swim together in a small, loosely associated herd or, in winter, groups of 20 or more may congregate around a warm spring. On such occasions they nuzzle and play and seem to enjoy one another's company.

The dugong generally resembles the manatee in size and shape, except that its tail is divided into flukes, while the manatee's is rounded and paddlelike. Dugongs inhabit Indo-Pacific waters from the Ryukyu Islands south of Japan to northern Australia and along the coasts of Mozambique and Madagascar. Some are found among the islands of the U. S. Pacific Trust territories.

The fate of sirenians today is precarious throughout their range. In many parts of the world, human activities have menaced the animals' survival. Even in protected areas they are still hunted for food. And their birth rate (usually one calf per cow every two or three years) may not be enough to prevent their eventual elimination from the roster of mammalian life.   HOWARD W. CAMPBELL

Manatee (*Trichechus manatus*)

The manatee still appears now and then in coastal waters from North Carolina to Texas, but its only stronghold in the United States is Florida. Scarcely a thousand of these placid mammals are left— remnant herds scattered along the state's Gulf and Atlantic shores.

Widely hunted in the past for their oil, hide, and meat, Florida's manatees face dangers of a different kind: collisions with powerboats and destruction of their habitat by urban development.

Small eyes and a droopy muzzle give the manatee a forlorn look. How well can it see and smell? No one knows. But it does hear well.

Manatees often communicate among themselves with a varied repertoire of squeaks, bleeps, and chirps.

Manatees lack leg and hip bones, but their front flippers retain vestigial nails and a handlike skeletal structure, reminders of a time when these animals lived

on land. Nor does the manatee use its flippers to swim. Its tail propels it, stroking powerfully up and down. The flippers are used mainly for close maneuvers—and to embrace during sexual congress.

Sea cows cannot stand cold water. During Florida's cool months they move southward, seeking the warmth of freshwater springs—and even

hot-water outlets from industrial plants. (The bull calf above, in a tattered coat of algae, shares his warm spot on the Crystal River with a school of gray snappers.)

Sea cows bear their young after a gestation of up to 400 days. Calves average 50 pounds (23 kg) at birth and suckle for two years.

Like a blimp in midair, a manatee hangs suspended in its element. Sea cows surface for air every two to five minutes but can hold their breath up to 20 minutes at rest. Valved nostrils seal out water when they dive. Dense, ivorylike bones enable them to stay submerged with minimal effort.

Hoofed Mammals

Order Artiodactyla

In the bone-nourishing velvet of summer, a white-tailed buck grows antlers that will take him through autumn's rut—testing time for him, a time of renewal for his kin in the order Artiodactyla.

America is a land of giants. After the dinosaurs died and the mammals arose, great beasts again roamed the land. Travelers across the land bridge that at times connected Alaska with Asia, they came from abroad or originated in this hemisphere and spread to the Old World. A wanderer through the ages could tell us of unbelievable creatures that once lived here, of the great extinctions and the turmoil of invasions as the bridge rose and fell with the pulse of glaciations.

That is certainly true of the order Artiodactyla, the cloven-hoofed mammals—no less so than other orders. Bizarre colossi—multi-horned relatives of deer with slingshot projections on their snouts, camels more than 10 feet tall, piglike animals as big as cows—ranged the continent. In the fossil record, the artiodactyls are found back to the beginning of the age of mammals. They proliferated into many lineages and showed their greatest abundance in the cooler, drier epochs preceding the Ice Ages, when grasslands spread over much of North America.

The giants are still here. Take almost any large mammal that Eurasia shares with North America and you will find the largest form on New World soil. The Siberian moose is large, but the Alaskan moose is larger. The giant among reindeer, the Osborn caribou, dwells in the Cassiar Mountains of British Columbia. Eurasia has many species of Old World deer; only one penetrated into North America—the elk, or wapiti, the giant of the tribe. So it goes, not only with contemporary animals but also with extinct forms. The largest bear, lion, saber-toothed tiger, wolf, bison, goat-antelope, elephant, horse, beaver—and on and on—is found in the fossil record or is still alive in North America.

The appearance of giants on this continent is not difficult to understand. A large animal

has proportionately less skin surface in relation to body volume than does a small animal. In cold climates this makes large size an advantage for retaining body heat.

When two members of a species compete for food, the larger one can usually find more to eat. And as a large mammal species disperses and colonizes new regions, the animals' new-found plenty tends to make them grow even bigger. We find, in the course of an evolutionary radiation, that small-bodied forms that develop in the tropics spin off increasingly larger-bodied and more grotesque forms as they invade progressively colder or drier environments.

North America, as an adjunct to the Eurasian land mass with a periodic northerly connection, would receive mainly giants adapted to cold and dryness. Had the Bering land bridge been at a lower latitude, the fauna here would be much more similar to that of Asia than is the case today.

It is also easy to understand why giants have such a high rate of extinction. They generally are ecological specialists, and therefore much more sensitive to ecological changes than smaller, more primitive, broadly adapted species. Such smaller animals have the best record of survival. Fossil beds are filled with the bones of extinct giants.

The severest slash to the American fauna came at the end of the last glaciation. We call it the megafaunal extinction. And we still argue about its cause (page 383). Was it climate? Was it man?

This background of evolutionary development is necessary for an understanding of the peculiar pattern of occurrence of artiodactyls in North America today. The order is composed of three suborders, all very distantly—if at all—related. They are Suiformes, which includes pigs, peccaries, and hippos;

the Tylopoda, containing the camels and llamas; and the Ruminantia, encompassing the deer, giraffes, bovines, pronghorns, and mouse deer. Altogether some 170 species occur, with representatives of the order on all continents except Australia and Antarctica.

Ironically, the camel and the horse (order Perissodactyla) originated in the Americas. Very late in their evolutionary history they entered Eurasia and Africa, and then became mysteriously extinct in their homeland.

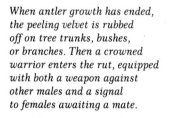

When antler growth has ended, the peeling velvet is rubbed off on tree trunks, bushes, or branches. Then a crowned warrior enters the rut, equipped with both a weapon against other males and a signal to females awaiting a mate.

After the rut is over, the antlers drop off. In spring new growth begins (opposite) from bone stumps called pedicels. Antlers differ in structure from horns, which are permanent projections.

When Jefferson Davis, as Secretary of War, imported some camels for Army use in the Southwest before the Civil War, stockmen were astonished at the animals' appetite for such local plants as creosote bush and manzanita, which other livestock spurned.

Camels did not survive the prejudice of mule skinners and ranchers who shot them. Horses and burros, however, survived in a feral state and flourished as true natives. Which, of course, they are—natives reintroduced from Europe (page 367). They were living in North America long before such species as the bighorn sheep came here.

Bighorns came from eastern Siberia; only on our continent has this northern, arctic form penetrated deep into the south. Desert bighorns are found from Nevada and California into Mexico. But when a true "desert" sheep—the Barbary sheep—was introduced from Africa into New Mexico (page 372), it readily accepted dry wasteland regions, where now the bighorn barely hangs on.

Artiodactyla means "having an even number of toes." And an even number of weight-bearing toes is one of the few things that members of the order have in common. A unique ankle joint and a foot structure based on development of the third and fourth digits (toes) carry the weight of the animal. This evolved as a means of handling the stress generated during running. The harder the ground and the higher the speed and the heavier the weight of the animal, the simpler and more elegant the foot structure became.

The horse's weight is carried by the third digit—a single hoof. In the artiodactyls, two digits do the work. This results in a symmetrical foot which has two main hoofs and often two small side hoofs, or dewclaws.

The megafaunal extinction left North America with only four families of artiodactyls. They are the Cervidae, the deer tribe; the Bovidae, hollow-horned animals that include bighorn sheep, mountain goats, and bison; the Antilocapridae, or pronghorns, which are truly American natives; and the Tayassuidae, or peccaries, small piglike creatures of American origin.

Except for the peccaries, all belong to the suborder of ruminants. Members of this suborder have a sophisticated digestive system, which enables them to exploit plant cellulose for energy. No mammal has enzymes capable of digesting cellulose; the ruminants culture microorganisms—bacteria and protozoa—to do it for them. These organisms grow within the rumen, an organ where fodder ferments by bacterial action. Fermentation

In the first snowfall of winter young bull elk spar and posture, performing a continual and ritualistic test of strength. Duels for dominance regulate social rank among hoofed mammals.

produces fatty acids and other products which enter the animal's bloodstream directly from the rumen. Then the bacteria and residue from the fodder go into the stomach and gut, where the bacteria are digested to further supply the ruminant's protein, mineral, and vitamin requirements.

Most true ruminants have some kind of hornlike organ sprouting from their heads. The projections may be ossicones—permanent bone cones covered by dense skin and hair, as in giraffes. They may be a tough horn covering a bony core—permanent and increasing by a segment each year, as in the bighorn. Or they may be bone structures grown and shed yearly, as are deer antlers. Horns and antlers serve as weapons of attack

and defense, and for display purposes. They may be luxury organs, in the best sense of the word. The better an animal is at getting the most nutritious food, the more it can spare from pure body needs.

The excess can be put into luxuries, into status—as big horns. Thus horns become symbols of prowess and ability. They say that physiologically this is indeed a very capable animal and a very good forager. Since the male with the biggest horns will breed with the most females, his traits will be passed on to more offspring.

But there's another side to having the biggest horns. My studies with mountain sheep have shown that rams with the largest luxury organs—the most dominant, the most virile,

the most successful individuals—have shorter lives. The same probably holds true among other ungulates—hoofed mammals. Such males exhaust themselves fighting and in rutting activities and mating. The result is that the less active, less prosperous male has the longest life expectancy.

Why do the females of some species have horns? Among ungulates that live together in large herds, females often look like males—so much so that even seasoned biologists may be fooled. One theory is that since the female must compete for forage at times against young males, she assumes their image. Another reason the females may have evolved horns is to discourage courting and harassing advances by young males, which tend to stay with the females after the rutting season. On the tundra, caribou cows grow antlers equal in size to those of three-year-old bulls. But among some of the more solitary woodland caribou, up to 40 percent of the females do not have antlers. Female elk don't grow antlers, but they do have manes and are nearly as large as the bulls.

If antlers are so important, why are they shed? Bucks busy sparring, fighting, and courting during the rutting season have little time to forage. After the rut they are exhausted, weakened, and vulnerable. Antlers make them stand out from the females; therefore, it's likely that predators would quickly learn that such standouts can be easy prey. Thus bucks have evolved the trait of shedding bone growth in order to look like just one of the crowd. Male mule deer not only slough their antlers but also mimic female actions—even crouching to urinate.

Another strategy for avoiding predators after the rut would be to go into hiding. And that is what the male blacktail and mule deer do. Bull elk do too, for a time. But then they form their own groups, separate from the females. At that time, however, the males need their antlers to maintain their dominance hierarchy. Consequently, they don't cast off their racks until warm weather.

In the north, bull elk barely have enough time to grow and harden a new set before another rutting season begins. But for elk populations established farther south—the tule elk of California, for example—the seasons have so spread that males begin to rut while their new antlers still are in velvet.

Strategies against predators involve more than just the shedding of antlers. Take the

case of the mule deer and the whitetail. Both may share the same habitat. But the whitetail is a hider; it favors dense brush, and if discovered it erupts from cover with a crash, then dashes off. It runs as fast as possible, trying to get so far ahead of pursuers that its scent may evaporate and dim the trail. Or it will run through water or swampy spots to avoid leaving a trace of scent. It also likes to run where other deer may be lurking—and let someone else get chased for awhile. Such habits make for a nervous, fidgety species.

The mule deer pussyfoots around in the brush, coolly trying to stay hidden. If flushed, it "stots"—jumps straight up and possibly changes direction. While the whitetail prefers to rush downhill (letting gravity help add to its speed), the mule deer likes to bound uphill. This lets it gain elevation comparatively easily while the predator is forced to clamber up at far greater cost of energy. It also enables the mule deer to leap over a boulder or bush; the pursuer has to go around.

Bounding also permits the deer, with each jump, to depart in a totally unpredictable direction. But with the predator close at hand, the deer must not jump until the last possible moment. Otherwise, the pursuer can redirect itself. Such escape techniques call for coolness in timing—and make for a calm, collected type. Thus, as one offshoot, tranquil mule deer can be tamed with ease. Jittery whitetails cannot.

In tundra country or on open plains with scant cover, a lone newborn calf can be particularly vulnerable to predators. But if many young are around, their numbers swamp the enemy; a few calves may be taken by predators, but a lot live. So genetic selection among such herding mammals as the caribou has made for females that not only all reach a breeding state at the same time but also give birth almost en masse.

Among species whose young instinctively hide, such as the white-tailed deer, females give birth at different times. This reduces the risk that predators, taking one easy prey, will learn to expect to find others. Among such

"hiders," the birthing span tends to spread. So does the rutting season. Warm climates—with milder conditions for the vulnerable newborn and longer periods of nourishing vegetation—present more opportunities for rutting and giving birth. In such regions, females readily extend the birth season.

Except for pronghorns, single young are the rule among animals that live in herds and run for their lives. The larger the young, the more likely it will be able to outrun predators.

Still shedding its long-haired coat of winter, a mountain goat clambers up a steep slope of its lofty habitat. Hoofs (left) with a hard outer edge for digging in and a tough, rubbery inner pad for traction make the goat at home on cliff edge, crag, or smooth rock. Members of the order Artiodactyla have feet designed so that two toes carry the weight. Adaptation produces variations, such as the caribou's spreading hoof, which is suited for travel over soft ground.

And it will grow out of its dangerous juvenile period faster if it does not have to compete with a sibling for the mother's milk. The baby gnu of Africa is a classic example; five or ten minutes after birth it can keep up with a herd that is running 25 miles an hour.

While the ungulate mother bears and cares for her young, the father contributes only his genes. Therefore, this contribution should come from a superior male. To be fit, one must maintain access to resources, particularly when they are scarce. Fighting over resources can be costly in time and energy, to say nothing of the danger from horn or hoof. The cheapest way of maintaining access is to establish dominance over competing individuals. Then the most dominant animal gets

A caribou calf a few days old trots after its mother across the arctic tundra. Northern animals that travel in herds have their young—one big baby for each mother—at the same time, virtually on the run. Scattered births or litters would give predators an easier and a steadier diet.

the biggest share and the other animals get progressively less.

A male ungulate's ultimate aim, of course, is access to the female. Some ungulates— such as mule deer and moose—are sequentially polygamous: The male stays with one female until she is bred, then he leaves her for another. In contrast, elk bucks herd females together into harems for mating.

The bull elk advertises. He bugles. He tries to out-bugle his competitors, and if one advertises nearby, he goes and shuts him up or chases him off. The bigger the elk's body, the more resonance his call has. So the females cluster to the bull with the deeper voice and the one that other bulls can't shut up.

But fighting for dominance among ungulates can cause serious wounds, even death. The sharp horns of mountain goats jab and puncture, and the males have evolved a tough shield—hide an inch thick—on their rumps, where the most blows land in their side-to-side, head-to-haunch type of fighting. Even so, deep wounds result.

The elk charges with sharp polished antlers; punctures and broken necks may occur. Bighorns clash head on. They have evolved multi-roofed skulls, tough facial skin, and incredibly sturdy neck tendons to withstand tremendous impact. Moose can kick from both ends. A bull moose, using its hind legs, struck a man standing on a corral chute eight feet above the ground.

Injury to the victor, however, may be as severe as to the vanquished. So real fights are infrequent. Instead, ungulates have adopted more subtle methods which aim at the same establishment of superiority but are not as costly. They are called dominance displays.

Essentially, display occurs when an animal shows off its weapons without making a move to use them. Threats, on the contrary, bring weapons into readiness. Deer that rise on hind legs to flail may threaten by lifting the head or forebody, raising a leg, or stamping the ground. The cow elk that bites will pull back her lips and grind her teeth. Or a dominant bighorn ram threatens an inferior competitor by jerking his horns downward in order to frighten him. But to a serious rival he displays his horns with his head drawn up and back so that his neck muscles bulge. Thus, the opponent may judge his power.

The displays of most large mammals show off the mass of their bodies. To display, these animals turn broadside and erect specialized hair, such as hair of the mane or along the spine. They call attention to distinctive markings and make themselves appear as large and conspicuous as possible.

The red deer, close relative of the elk, enhances the size of his antlers by horning shrubbery and collecting vegetation on his rack, so it looks larger. During the rut, the bull elk urinates on his underbody, then wallows in wet soil. The mud darkens the animal along his entire length, including the mane, making him more impressive.

But it isn't enough just to display, display. The dominant animal has to have credibility: Now and then he has to back up his threats with force. The ultimate credibility is a test of strength. It pays the dominant animal to reinforce his position periodically—and the subordinate animal to test the dominant's competence from time to time. So sparring, even serious fighting, results.

Interestingly, mule deer form social bonds as a result of sparring matches. A superior may handle a lesser male in successive bouts and lord it over him afterwards, but let the subordinate be harassed by other lesser males, and the superior comes to the rescue.

Sparring and fights both are ended by the subordinate's breaking off with some submissive act. Pretending—with exaggerated motions—to graze is an almost universal signal among hoofed animals that says, "Look, I'm really peaceful." Often the submission takes the form of acting like a female.

Thus the effect of weapons, the ability to learn, the preference of individuals to live in a social milieu where roles are understood and played out—all this combines to create a dominance hierarchy we can recognize. They sometimes act like us.   VALERIUS GEIST

Family Tayassuidae

Peccaries aren't pigs, but superficially the animals are look-alikes. The two families began going their separate ways some 40 to 70 million years ago when the pigs (family Suidae) developed in the Eastern Hemisphere and the peccaries mainly in the west. Thus, in North America today both the domestic hog and the wild boar (*Sus scrofa*) are introduced "exotics."

The less obvious differences between pigs and peccaries are considerable. Peccaries have fewer teeth than most pigs (38 to a pig's 44) and have partially fused foot bones, an adaptation for running. Peccaries' shorter, straighter tusks fit so closely that they hone each other to razor sharpness with each snap of the jaws. These spear-edged weapons give peccaries a common name, javelina.

Peccaries are more herbivorous than pigs and have a more complex stomach for digesting coarsely chewed food. One favorite of the collared peccary: cactus, especially the prickly pear, which is eaten spines and all.

The family's three species—placed in two genera—range from the southwestern United States to central South America.

Peccaries have on their rumps glands that give out a fluid with a strong, musky odor. Early observers of the "musk hog" mistook the gland for a navel.

Collared Peccary (*Dicotyles tajacu*)

These peccaries usually live out their lives in social groups of five to 15, though some, old and infirm, may die in solitude. There are no harems or bachelor groups. The herd sleeps, forages, and eats together.

But there are squabbles. Adversaries square off, lay back their ears, and clatter their canines at each other. In fights they charge head on, bite, and occasionally lock jaws.

Scent from the rump gland is a cohesive of the herd. The scent marks the home range and helps herd individuals identify each other. Peccaries rub against rocks, stumps, and tree trunks, leaving smears of the oily fluid. They also rub against each other, standing head to rump. This is apparently a form of greeting, not a sexual ritual.

There is no certain breeding season. Young, usually twins, are born about 144 days after mating. When mature, they weigh 30 to 60 pounds (14 to 27 kg).

D. tajacu ranges from southern Arizona, New Mexico, and Texas into northern Argentina.

These twins will follow mother past their first year; as infants, they sheltered beneath her, their purring answered by grunts.

Family Cervidae

Long-legged and graceful, delicate or formidable, North American members of the Cervidae, the deer family, range from tiny Key deer of Florida to huge Alaskan moose. Males of all American species, and caribou females, carry antlers. These grow rapidly in summer—soft, tender bone covered with a thin skin whose fine hairs look like velvet (as the moose, right, is wearing). When growth stops, the skin dries and is rubbed off. Later, a ring of cells breaks down bone at the base; antlers drop—to weather away or be gnawed by mineral-hungry rodents. Antler growth depends a great deal upon the animal's health; the number of antler points does not indicate a deer's age.

Like other artiodactyls, deer have fused metacarpal and metatarsal bones—structures analogous to human palm and instep bones—which form the shock-resistant "cannon bone" of the lower leg.

The deer family originated in the Old World about 40 million years ago. But some species that evolved on this continent, often called the New World deer, have a relatively primitive foot equipped with well-developed dewclaws and elastic hoofs, ideal for soft ground and for climbing. North American species live in forests, upland deserts, swamps, and tundra. Old World members, as well as their North American counterpart, the elk—or wapiti—have hoofs better suited for hard ground.

Elk or Wapiti (*Cervus elaphus*)

The two bull elk walking side by side break into a trot, then a run. Two hundred yards across the meadow they wheel and walk back. Several times they pace, sweeping antlers low to the ground at each turn. Glinting antlers and dark body parts catch the rival's eye to show off size and strength. Thus they duel for dominance.

Special brain cells—in animals as well as humans—react to sharp edges moving across the line of vision. Elk antlers present such sharp edges. But the antlers are not merely symbols; they

are sturdy enough to absorb a rival's thrust—and straight enough to prevent entanglement. Antlers rarely lock.

Elk are the most highly evolved of the Old World deer. They have adapted to open land, feeding on grasses as well as forest browse. The raised head helps an elk in the open spot a predator. The animal spends about one hour in seven standing or walking; the rest of the time, feeding or resting. So a group needs at least seven members as insurance that on the average one head will be up (as happens in the photo above).

Elk, called wapiti by Shawnee Indians, stand up to 5 feet (152 cm) at the shoulders and weigh as much as 1,100 pounds (500 kg).

The TULE ELK (*C.e. nannodes*), palest, smallest subspecies, weighs 325 to 400 pounds (147 to 181 kg). Its habitat is confined to a small area in east-central California.

Sunrise gilds an elk mother and her suckling. Birth—usually one young—is in spring. By four months a calf is weaned and unspotted.

Mule Deer (*Odocoileus hemionus*)

Bleating like a young deer in distress, a buck trots after a doe. He is trying to get near enough to coax her to urinate. Then he will sniff and curl his lip so that a nasal organ can analyze her urine; the level of hormones will tell whether the doe is ready to breed. But the doe has a genetic mission: to be selected by the fittest. And she skips along, retaining her urine. Now the buck tries another courtship strategy. With a sudden leap, a slap of the ground, and a horrible roar, he frightens her so much that she urinates. From such autumn rituals come in May, June, or July the birth of young, usually twins.

The mule deer gets its name from huge ears two-thirds the length of its head; they aid in detecting danger at long range. Mule deer are also called jumping deer because of their stotting—stiff-legged bounding with all four feet off the ground—when sensing danger. They can stot while standing or in flight.

Mule deer differ in individual body markings and coat colors. Tones range from a dark ash-gray or brown-gray to a light gray or browns and reds. Rump patches, which surround the short, slim, black-tipped tail, range from white to yellowish.

Mule deer forage for a wide array of foods. Twigs, leaves, and rotted or frost-killed plants are consumed in small bites. The deer may climb hard snowbanks to reach aspen catkins high above the ground.

Though its forebears predate the Ice Ages, the mule deer is a relatively recent and advanced offshoot of the genus. It has adapted to high elevations and semidesert regions, and can be found in broken country, chaparral, brush, and woods. Adult males vary in weight—from 180 to 400 pounds (82 to 181 kg)—and stand about 3.3 feet (101 cm) at the shoulder. Females are smaller.

Columbian Black-tailed Deer (*Odocoileus hemionus columbianus*)

One of eleven subspecies of *O. hemionus*, the Columbian blacktail haunts forested coastal regions from southern British Columbia to central California. Browsing on lush undergrowth, it seldom needs to drink.

This subspecies and the Sitka deer (*O.h. sitkensis*) are often called black-tailed deer, while the others are usually known as mule deer. Sitka deer live in British Columbia, Alaska's panhandle, and offshore islands.

In the mountainous eastern limits of its range, the Columbian blacktail breeds with mule deer. Typically, *O.h. columbianus*, with its distinctive brushlike tail, is darker and smaller than the muley. A blacktail buck stands about 3 feet (91 cm) at the shoulder; weight ranges from 110 to 250 pounds (50 to 113 kg). Does average about 100 pounds (45 kg).

While mule deer, adapting to progressively higher elevations and scattered forage, have extended

☐ Mule Deer
☐ Columbian Black-tailed Deer

their range across western North America, blacktails are found only in the Pacific Northwest.

Less social and more nocturnal than mule deer, and with localized migratory tendencies, blacktails in small bands have been observed defending territories against intruding deer. Thus, by not sharing the available food, they stand a better chance of surviving the winter. In defending an area, blacktails demonstrate individually and collectively the ability to recognize certain landmarks that define territories.

White-tailed Deer (*Odocoileus virginianus*)

Six veteran hunters combed the square mile of forest where 39 deer were fenced. It took the hunters four days to spot one buck. In another test, five men followed a buck wearing a radio collar and orange streamers on his ear tags. They took all day to find him hidden in the underbrush. Thus does the white-tailed deer merit its proverbial reputation as a hider—and survivor. For the animal that supplied buckskin and venison to a frontier nation still exists in great numbers: Urbanized Pennsylvania can sustain a yearly harvest of about 100,000—and some 25,000 more killed by cars.

Except for parts of the Southwest and California, whitetails range over most of the continent south of Hudson Bay. Some 20 subspecies live in the Nearctic. Northerners (such as the white-tailed buck and fawns above) look chunkier

Key Deer (*Odocoileus virginianus clavium*)

The young leave a hoofprint the size of a human thumbnail. The adults themselves grow no larger than an Irish Setter or German Shepherd. These are the Key deer, a diminutive subspecies of white-tailed deer.

Found only on the Florida Keys, they are protected as endangered animals. A few decades ago, their numbers had dwindled to 25 or 50. Now there are 350 to 400, but their habitat is encroached upon by humans, and about one a week is killed on a highway. A natural limitation—availability of fresh water—also checks their population. The Key deer has a reproductive rate lower than its kindred subspecies.

When Ice Age glaciers melted and seas rose, ancestors of the Key deer were stranded on the island chain and developed their distinctive size and an unusual tolerance for salt. They eat mangrove leaves and more than 160 other plants in their luxuriant habitat. Powerful swimmers, Key deer cross channels between islets to find ponds in dry seasons.

OVERLEAF: *"As swift as the roes upon the mountains," a buck bursts from cover, flicking the tail that named his species. He will dash to leave pursuers behind, then hide again.*

The whitetail's antlers sweep forward, single points branching up from the main beams. The rack of the mule deer grows more vertically and each beam has twinned branches.

because their coats are thicker than those of southern races. Tubular hairs give buoyancy for swimming. The coats' insulation enables the deer to lie on snow and not melt it. Most whitetails have reddish coats in summer.

Whitetails, also known as Virginia deer for the area where they were scientifically described, weigh some 200 pounds (91 kg) and measure about 6 feet (183 cm) from nose to tail. They forage on a wide variety of vegetation, including twigs, fungi, and shoots.

In a ritual of recognition, a
fawn nuzzles its mother, then
begins to suckle. Like other
deer, whitetails mate in
autumn. Does give birth, usually
to two young, in spring. Triplets
(opposite) occasionally occur;
they survive when deer are well
fed and in a relatively safe
place—here, a game farm.
   A spotted coat camouflages
the fawn in shade-dappled
thickets. For a few weeks after
birth it hides, withholding
feces and urine. Then the mother
ingests what the fawn voids,
denying predators a telltale scent.
The young grow quickly, fed on
milk with three times the protein
and fat of cows' milk.

Moose (*Alces alces*)

Least social of antlered species, this largest of the deer tribe leads a solitary life in woodlands of the north. The moose's name comes from the Algonquin for "he cuts or trims smooth." That moose do, browsing on twigs, leaves, bark, and shrubs. In summer they wade far out into ponds for water lilies. A massive head dips underwater so rubbery lips can pluck plants from the bottom. A big, sensitive muzzle sorts out, by feel, different foods. Bulky, high-shouldered bodies and long legs give moose an ungainly look. Yet they can speed through water—or snow—while pursuers flounder. Bull Alaskan moose may tower 7 feet (213 cm), weigh up to 1,800 pounds (816 kg). An exceptional rack of antlers may weigh 70 pounds (32 kg).

Males in rut "nasal test" females (as a bull apparently does above). Although males engage in head-to-head shoving matches for a mate, they are not always the pursuers. Cows lure them with grunting, mooing love calls, which hunters imitate with birch-bark horns. After eight months' gestation the mother gives birth to one young—sometimes twins. They run with her the first year.

A young moose walks safely before a mother formidable enough to keep a wolf at bay. Moose mothers are so aggressive and attentive that newborn do not have—nor do they need—protective spots.

OVERLEAF: *Wary eye cocked to a photographer at work, a moose cow comes up streaming water. Moose may dive as deep as 18 feet to feed on pondweed and water lily. Nostrils close during dives.*

Caribou (*Rangifer tarandus*)

In waves and in parallel lines like iron filings shaped by a magnet, the caribou move across the tundra. Their feet click as they move—like castanets—a characteristic shared by all caribou races. A group spurts ahead to a patch of green and pauses to graze. Others trot on. A stream may cause a bunching until some cow or bull takes the lead and swims across.

Thus do caribou of the tundra make their twice-yearly migrations: in one direction to calving grounds in the spring, then back again to winter ranges in the fall. Pastures may be 900 miles apart.

Most herds number in the thousands.

The species *R. tarandus* is split into a number of subspecies. Two of these, traditionally known as "barren-ground caribou," are *R. t. groenlandicus* in Canada and *R. t. granti* in Alaska.

Caribou feed on sedges, grasses, forbs, and willow and birch leaves. But lichens are the mainstay of their diet. They eat about 12 pounds a day, nibbling at the slow-growing plants with small, weak teeth. To find enough forage, they must

☐ *R. t. caribou* and others
☐ *R. t. groenlandicus*
☐ *R. t. granti*

be constantly on the move. Most of the year they roam in small bands of like sex or in loose herds of several hundred; these come together for migration.

Male caribou stand 4.2 feet (128 cm) at the shoulder and average 240 pounds (109 kg). Precocious calves are born singly but dropped within a few days of each other by all cows in the herd.

Spring calves stay close to cows as caribou begin fall migration. This herd totals more than 100,000.

Science Report

Due Date : March 11, 2003 Tuesday

We have been discussing different animals and what they do in the winter. Some animals hibernate. Other animals migrate. Then there are animals that adapt. Pick an animal from the list below. Go to the library and read about that animal. Please use at least two books from the library. Then complete the questions found in this report.

Here is a list of animals that you are to choose from. Please pick one animal to examine.

skunks	caribou	rabbits
birds	red fox	deer
beavers	squirrels	chipmunks

1. What is the name of the animal that you have chosen to research?
2. List two facts about the animal that you have researched.
3. What does the animal do in the winter? Does it hibernate, adapt, or migrate? Explain.
4. Write the titles of the books that you used to find your information.
5. Draw a detailed illustration of the animal that you have researched. The illustration should show what the animal you have researched does in the winter.

Woodland Caribou (*Rangifer tarandus caribou*)

This caribou lives up to its name, dwelling in boreal forests of aspen, spruce, and jack pine. Within this realm it migrates from boggy fens to drier ridges; the caribou of the tundra usually winter below the arctic tree line, wandering from stunted growth to open tundra. Caribou of the mountains migrate up and down, from high alpine tundra to low woody elevations. All these types—and the partly domesticated caribou, or reindeer, of northern Europe and Asia—belong to a single widespread genus and species, *Rangifer tarandus*.

Woodland and tundra caribou can be identified by their antlers. The woodland has flatter antlers with many short points. It is also larger and darker. Bulls of the Osborn caribou, largest of the genus, weigh up to 700 pounds (318 kg).

The woodland caribou's habitat makes it less gregarious than the tundra dwellers. Groups are small. In the rutting season, bucks may mate with up to a dozen or so does. The bucks shed their antlers shortly after the autumn rut; the antlers begin growing again in March. Females grow antlers in late summer and keep them until spring calving. This growth schedule gives pregnant does weapons and a chance for dominance as they dispute with young bucks over forage.

Like others of its kind, woodland caribou combat northern cold with an outer coat of long guard hairs and a fine, short underfur. Hollow guard hairs give added insulation and buoyancy; caribou are excellent swimmers. Hair covers nearly all the body of most caribou. The caribou of the tundra shed so much in summer that the discarded hair of a big herd piles up in windrows along the edges of lakes and streams.

Woodland caribou once were common in northern coniferous forests. Modern estimates put their numbers at 43,000.

Peary's Caribou (*Rangifer tarandus pearyi*)

☐ Peary's Caribou
☐ Woodland Caribou

On the island-dotted edges of the far north live the smallest of the caribou tribe—Peary's caribou, named for the explorer who encountered them within 500 miles of the Pole. They roam a land where scant food resources limit an animal's size.

This subspecies is slightly smaller than its cousins of the tundra, and its winter pelage is paler in color. Like the other subspecies of tundra and woodland, Peary's caribou scoops through snow with a forefoot to reach the vegetation beneath.

Caribou hoofs form a broad digging tool, an efficient paddle, and body support for soft terrain. Dewclaws are large and low so they carry some of the animal's weight. In summer, horny hoof edges are worn down, and fleshy inner pads are exposed for walking on marshy ground. In winter, the pads shrink and hair between the hoofs grows longer. The rims of the hoofs expand to provide traction on ice.

The clicking of caribou feet can be heard 30 yards away. Grazing companions find these reassuring sounds, because they are impossible for predator wolves to imitate. The clicking may be caused by snapping tendons or moving bones.

Family Antilocapridae

This family's name—*antilo* for antelope, *capri* for goat—misnames the family's sole species, the pronghorn. It is neither a true antelope nor a true goat. It is the last remnant of a group of bizarre spiral-horned and fork-horned mammals that arose in North America in the Eocene Epoch. Before settlers arrived, pronghorns dotted the plains by the millions. Far fewer now roam from southern Canada to northern Mexico, with greatest numbers in Montana and Wyoming.

Along with deer, bison, and other ruminants, the pronghorn has a four-part stomach, which acts as a fermentation vat. After eating, the animal regurgitates the softened cud for chewing, swallowing, and final digestion. Both sexes have horns (below), their sheaths shed annually. Specialized skin over a bony core produces first hair and then horn. Thus each year the "horn skin" renews the core's outer sheath.

Horn Sheath
"Horn Skin"
Bony Core

Pronghorn (*Antilocapra americana*)

A biologist who had been an army officer discovered that pronghorn bucks were good strategists: They staked out territories with short, easily defended borders. He also found that when the rut began, the complex, rigid system broke down and dominant bucks vanished—along with does in heat. The biologist found that dominant males had hiding places where they held females for mating. Young bucks could not find them. And, no trysting place, no does.

When courting, a male offers a female a sniff of glands under patches of black hair below the ear (as above). The glands give off

a powerful secretion that helps to identify him and mark territory.

The biggest pronghorns, adult males, stand about 3 feet (91 cm) at the shoulders and weigh 90 to 150 pounds (41 to 68 kg). Bucks' horns average 12 inches (30 cm); does' are shorter than their ears and lack "prongs." Some females have no horns.

Does breed at about 16 months of age and usually bear twins. The young grow rapidly. When only four or five days old, they can outrun a man.

A high reproductive rate has helped the pronghorn recover from a low of about 15,000 in 1910 to today's 500,000. A dweller of the dry plains and semidesert, it combats cold and heat with its body hairs. They are hollow and can lie flat to insulate or be lifted to let air circulate. The white hairs of its rump patch can be raised as a warning signal visible two and a half miles away.

OVERLEAF: *Pronghorns, fastest North American mammals, race through a speed-blurred world. They can run for short spurts at over 50 miles an hour and cruise at 25 or 30.*

Family Bovidae

Bison stringing through Yellowstone
snows (right)... mountain goats clinging
to a lofty crag... Jersey cows munching in
a dairyman's barn—all belong to the
family Bovidae. This great array of hoofed
mammals provides us with some of our most
spectacular wildlife and some of our most
valuable farm animals, domesticated about
8,000 or 9,000 years ago.

Almost all bovids have horns, usually
borne by both sexes. Dewclaws normally are
small or missing. Members of most species
live gregariously. Bison and muskoxen
exhibit contagious behavior in grazing and
movement. All bovids are ruminants, able
to regurgitate food and chew it a second
time. Those that feed on grass pull it
rather than bite it off, to get at the tender
lower stems. Although most family members
are grassland dwellers, some species
are found in desert, mountains, and tundra.

Bison (*Bison bison*)

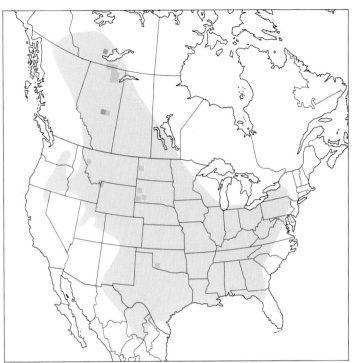

☐ Bison's Historic Range
■ Wood Buffalo Herds
▨ Park and Refuge Herds

In three hours this brand-new bison will run with a species that almost died. Today bison roam in protected herds. For preservation purposes, Canada has isolated its wood buffalo. They had been breeding with plains bison and disappearing as a race.

A large bison bull may stand six feet at the shoulder and weigh a ton. His massive weight is concentrated in his forequarters, his heavily muscled neck supports a low-hung head, and his matted forelock hair forms a thick shock absorber known to have stopped bullets.

A bull can push a one-ton opponent backward 10 to 15 feet. And when two bulls charge, the spectacle is awesome. Usually they first roll in shallow wallows—horn-dug through the sod, the subsoil churned to flourlike dust. They posture and paw the ground. And then the dust explodes as they lunge at each other from a few feet apart—and collide.

Deep, bellowing roars accompany such fights. John James Audubon,

camped on the plains in 1843, noted that the din of the numerous conflicts sounded like "the long continued roll of a hundred drums."

Hooking horns rip out hunks of hair. Wounds—and death—occur. But usually the clashes end when one bull turns his head or body aside in submission, recognition of the rival's dominance.

Fights occur mostly during rut in late summer and early fall. Until then bulls have wandered alone or in small groups on the periphery of larger bands of females and subadults. The bands roam together loosely as a herd.

In rutting season, the bulls join the bands, busily competing with rivals and tending one cow after another until each is mated. A bull may lose 300 pounds during the rut. Calves are born in spring after a gestation of about nine months.

Adult animals lose some of their distinctive foreleg "pantaloons" and other display hair after the rut. Sexes then are quite similar in appearance, though females are smaller—averaging 5 feet (152 cm) and 930 pounds (422 kg)—with slenderer horns whose tips point forward. (Bulls' curve upward.)

Plains bison, misnamed buffalo by European settlers, use their ranges erratically. No firm evidence supports former belief that they migrated extreme distances north and south with the seasons. Herds may seek winter shelter of tree belts in storms, or move to better forage in snow—sweeping muzzles like brooms to dig down as deep as four feet for food.

Once bison ranged almost all the continent. To Plains Indians they were a four-legged commissary, yielding "meat, drink, shoes, houses, fire, vessels, and their Masters whole substance," an explorer wrote. Hunters on the plains after the Civil War virtually exterminated them. Today plains bison number about 50,000.

The WOOD BUFFALO (*Bison bison athabascae*) exists in two small herds in Canada. It is larger, darker, and more wary than the plains bison.

OVERLEAF: *Few where once there were millions, bison thunder across plains their ancestors ruled. Bison can run 32 miles an hour in short bursts.*

Mountain Goat (*Oreamnos americanus*)

Mountain lions may corner it in a cave when it seeks shelter at night or in a storm. Wolves may pounce on it when it descends to wooded valleys and alpine meadows. Eagles may swoop down and seize its kids. But when the mountain goat takes to its lofty realm, few foes dare to follow. (Safely gamboling on the high pass

above are, from the left, an adult female, two adult males, and a leaping youngster.)

The scientific name suggests that the Greek Oreiad, a nymph of the mountains, has been reborn in America. But the common name offers a zoological error, for

O. americanus is not a true goat. It belongs to the goat-antelope group that has adapted to life on the crags. It is kin to the chamois of the Alps and came here from Eurasia in an early Ice Age. Up to 100,000 now can be found in remote high country in northwestern states, Alaska, and western Canada, where most live.

The mountain goat has a body built for climbing: flexible hoofs; compact, muscular torso; rather short legs—poor for running but ideal for balance.

Males and females, including yearlings, have stiletto horns that can deeply puncture even the tough skin of the male's rump shields, which thicken during rut. Natural selection has led to aggressive, horn-wielding females that zealously guard their kids and dominate males except during rut.

Courting males crawl on their bellies and squeak tenderly like baby goats to win a nanny. After mating, the billy prudently leaves—or gets chased away.

On a diet of grasses, sedges, and shrubs, males grow to an average 3.5 feet (107 cm) in shoulder height and weigh from 190 to 280 pounds (86 to 127 kg). Females weigh about a third less.

Muskox (*Ovibos moschatus*)

Despite *ovibos*—"sheep ox"—and *moschatus*—"musky"—of its scientific name, this animal is neither sheep nor ox nor musky. Its misnomer may stem from the odor of urine on bulls in rut; muskoxen have no musk glands.

Confronted by an intruder, they move with an instinct born of the ages. The herd forms itself into a defensive ring (as above), massive heads facing out, calves protected in the center, behind the furry rampart. If the intruder steps closer, an adult will rush out to meet the threat with a goring or trampling.

Such tactics, developed through millenniums of battle with wolves, worked against those predators. But that behavior meant suicide in contests with human hunters, especially the ones bearing guns. An entire herd of muskoxen might be shot where it stood.

Once these Ice Age relics roamed with mastodon, hairy mammoth, and woolly rhinoceros, but they had been exterminated in Eurasia in prehistoric times. In North America in 1689 Henry Kelsey became the first of many explorers to see the "ill shapen beast. . . . their Hair is near a foot long."

In the 1850's Alaska saw its last muskox killed. Thousands in Canada were slaughtered to meet demands of the lap-robe trade.

Muskoxen were so rare by 1917 that Canada ordered total protection. Their numbers have since recovered to about 25,000; herds have been re-established in some former ranges.

During the rut, bulls that have been solitary or in bachelor bands rejoin groups of females and younger animals. Herds usually average around 15 members and may number as many as 100. Bulls are polygamous and compete for mates. Two rivals may charge each other repeatedly in head-on clashes until one concedes.

Though clumsy looking, muskoxen are nimble. Bulls measure about 4.5 feet (137 cm) at the shoulder and weigh an average of 750 to 800 pounds (340 to 363 kg). Females are smaller and their horns are less broad.

Muskoxen roam river valleys, lakeshores, and damp meadows in the summer, feeding on willows, sedges, and grasses. They do not particularly like lichens, the caribou's chief food, and so the two species can share the same range. In winter, muskoxen move to hilltops, slopes, and plateaus, where the wind helps clear the vegetation of snow. They survive on a sixth of the fodder needed by domestic cattle.

Bitter cold following wet snow may turn the crust to concrete hardness; unable to paw through to forage, muskoxen starve.

Dangling guard hairs—as long as 24 inches (61 cm) on a bull's neck—shed moisture. Underneath, a dense, downy layer of wool finer than cashmere turns away cold. Shed in April or May, it trails after the animal in streamers, or clings in patches to tundra shrubs and plants.

To Eskimos the animal was *Oomingmak*—"bearded one." They wove mosquito nets from the guard hairs. *Qiviut* they call the gossamer-light, incredibly warm underwool. A pound of it can be spun into a strand 10 miles long; four ounces is enough to knit a dress. A muskox yields about six pounds of the wool, and for it ranchers hope to domesticate the adaptable, mild-tempered animal.

Dall's Sheep (*Ovis dalli*)

Wary when hunted, Dall's sheep will flee at a hint of danger. But where they are protected they will accept and even approach humans. (The males above cluster to stare inquisitively at the photographer.)

The wild sheep's ability to get used to human beings may explain why sheep became domesticated very early in our prehistoric past.

Dall's rams banding together demonstrate a trait of mountain sheep behavior. After the rut, males leave herds of ewes and juveniles to roam in small bands. They move from one grazing patch to another in a pattern set during interglacial periods, when climate changes shrank the grasslands their ancestors roamed.

Good grazing patches may be 40 miles apart, and elders know the routes through the valleys that stitch the patches together. Young males cannot go off on their own because they have not learned the way. So they must tag along.

But how does a youngster stay out of harm's way among big, aggressive rams? He imitates females. This behavior redirects aggression by the dominant rams, allowing the smaller, weaker animal to stay in male company.

Stone's Sheep (*Ovis dalli stonei*)

Stone's sheep, a thin-horn, has been called "a Dall's sheep in evening dress." The white of rump, belly, head, and leg trim contrasts with the silver-gray through brown to near-black of its body.

As with other mountain sheep, a Stone's ewe bred in autumn's rut bears her lamb in spring. She seeks a cliff or the isolation of broken country to give birth and there cement maternal bonds. In an experiment, ewes failed to pick their own from lambs tied in bags and presented headfirst. But when the bags were reversed, the ewes had no problem. Anal glands made the difference. In a herd, a mother will nurse only her own. But a female with no lamb of her own may become what author Geist calls an "aunty" that young flock around.

Young males join roaming ram bands after their second birthday. Young females stay with the herd.

Stone's head-to-tail measure of about 5.3 feet (162 cm) makes it longer-bodied than Dall's sheep. It also is somewhat heavier.

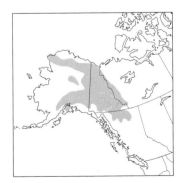

☐ Dall's Sheep
☐ Stone's Sheep

Dall's sheep belong to the "thin-horn" branch of *Ovis*. Their horns spread and spiral more than the bighorn's; tips point away from the face. Males average about 3 feet (91 cm) in shoulder height and weigh from 165 to 200 pounds (75 to 91 kg). Grasses and sedges form their principal food.

Bighorn Sheep (*Ovis canadensis*)

Among *Ovis* species, horn size forms a symbol of rank. In the dominance hierarchy, the bigger the horns, the more dominant the owner. A ram's horns may weigh 30 pounds (14 kg), as heavy as all the bones of his body. The horns of an old ram (above) can be a biography. The horns are blunted and frayed at the tips, evidence of repeated bouts with his rivals. Ringing the horns are deep grooves—marks formed each autumn when annual growth stops. These show him to be about 10 years old; 14 is long-lived. Segments between creases narrow toward the base as growth slows with age and as each increment pushes older growth outward.

Butting jousts may occur all year but intensify during rut when rams join herds and vie for mates. Two rivals will rear on hind legs, then drop to all fours and slam together head on. The shock waves ripple through their bodies. Recovering, each freezes for up to a minute in a show-off of horns. Thus the blow received is instantly equated with the size of the horns that inflicted it.

For battle protection, mountain sheep have double-layered skulls shored with struts of bone. A broad, massive tendon linking skull

Suckling bighorn depends upon its mother for sustenance. But it assumes independence early, going off to gambol with other lambs. Play strengthens its limbs and body for life on the ledge.

and spine helps the head pivot and recoil at the blow.

A ram may weigh 250 to 280 pounds (113 to 127 kg) and measure 5.5 feet (168 cm) from head to tail. It can smash into an opponent at 20 miles an hour.

O. canadensis is found in the Rocky Mountains from southern Canada to Colorado, and as desert subspecies south into Mexico. Threatened with eventual extinction, it numbers about one-tenth of the population that existed when white people first began exploiting the Rockies. But the bighorn's social traditions dim hopes of recovery.

Unlike moose and white-tailed deer, whose young disperse and colonize new areas, mountain sheep young follow their elders. The bighorn is also imperiled by poachers for meat and horns, by diseases, by competition from livestock, and by continual human encroachment on habitats.

Adults seem to adjust to such pressures by holding down populations. The more restricted the habitat or the more scant the forage, the less viable the young and the smaller the herd.

The predominant bighorn of the desert, Ovis canadensis nelsoni, *is smaller than its northern cousin and has flatter, wider-spreading horns.*

The desert bighorn can be found in slightly varying forms from Nevada and California (left)—with a few in west Texas (above)—into Mexico. It inhabits hot, dry, rocky, cliff-and-mountain regions where its leanness gives it a large surface-to-weight ratio beneficial in getting rid of body heat.

Like other mountain sheep, desert bighorns aren't as well built for clambering as mountain goats. But bighorns can zigzag up and down cliff faces with apparent ease. A two-inch ledge is enough for a foothold, and a spot too small for a stand may be a place for a pause in a bounce from niche to niche over spans as wide as 20 feet.

These bighorns get moisture from desert plants. Though they need water, it may be several days between visits to water holes.

Rams stand 35 inches (89 cm) at the shoulder, weigh about 200 pounds (91 kg). Their rut season—July to October—is the longest of any mountain sheep. But single young and social traditions keep populations small. Competitors in the desert—wild burros and people—threaten the sheep's future.

OVERLEAF: *With a crack so loud it can be heard a mile away, two rams clash in Alberta's wilds. Rivals may butt repeatedly in a stylized ritual. Author Geist watched a determined pair collide some five times an hour for 25½ hours before one finally conceded.*

Alien Mammals

Introduced Species

Rhesus monkey business along Florida's Silver Springs River goes on in social groups, as it would in native India. The feral animals are descended from unemployed 1930's movie monkeys.

In January 1494 Christopher Columbus wrote home from Hispaniola. Half his men were sick, he told his sovereigns. "Under God," he said, "the preservation of their health depends on these people being provided with the food they are used to in Spain." Ferdinand and Isabella sent supplies and livestock. Such shipments from Spain began the introduction of exotic—nonnative—animals to the New World. Some survive only as domestic stock. Others have established wild populations which often endanger native plants and animals. Although today we try to control or forbid by law the importation of foreign species, our past record has been thoughtless and often catastrophic.

Columbus supposedly left swine on Hispaniola when he went home in 1496, and their descendants, transported to the mainland, were probably the first pigs in North America. In 1521 hogs were penned aboard the ships that Juan Ponce de Leon sailed to Florida. Hernando de Soto, in 1539, brought 13 hogs to the North American mainland. According to expedition journals, they "increased to three hundred swine." Escapees from Spanish herds were perhaps ancestors of the wild hogs that are now found in the southeastern United States.

The horse, unlike the pig, was here long before Columbus, as *Hyracotherium*—often known as *Eohippus,* "dawn horse" of the Eocene—some 55 million years ago and, about three million years ago, as its descendant, *Equus,* the genus to which the modern horse belongs. *Equus* prospered until about 8,000 years ago when, along with other large mammals, it vanished from the continent. Ecologist Paul S. Martin believes that this massive extinction was not the result of climatic changes but the work of Stone Age hunters who slaughtered many species out of exis-

tence. "The complete removal of North American horses," he says, "... represents the loss of a lineage of grass-eaters, without the loss of the grass! It left the horse niche empty for at least eight thousand years."

The Spanish brought this lineage of grass-eaters back. From breeding farms in the West Indies conquistadores picked up pack animals and fine mounts. Francisco Coronado had more than 500 with him when he encountered Plains Indians in 1541.

At first, the Indians probably feared the horse. But, a Cree warrior said, "as he was a slave to man, like the dog, which carried our things, he was named the Big Dog." Although no one knows when the first mounted Indian proudly rode off on his Big Dog, horse ownership grew among the tribes through trading and raiding, and by 1800 the Plains Indian was transformed from a foot-stalker to a swift and skillful mounted hunter.

Another *Equus* species, the burro, followed the conquistadores and eventually scattered to the wild after having served as beast of burden all over the American West. Today both horses and burros roam in feral herds. Are they "living symbols of the historic and pioneer spirit of the West"? So says the 1971 Act of Congress that protects those on public lands from "capture, branding, harassment, or death." Or are these animals ecological misfits, intruders in niches belonging properly to other wildlife?

By the 1960's the native bighorn sheep had almost disappeared from several areas of California because, state biologists believe, the booming burro population competes with the sheep for forage and water. A game official accuses burros of "competing with every living animal on the desert, right down to salamanders at the water holes"—where burros trample the ground enough to destroy habitat for many kinds of small animals. At Grand Canyon National Park, rangers shot 2,800 burros between 1924 and 1969 to protect native plants and animals. Although the shooting has stopped, some 350 burros remain in the canyon, and they are increasing at the rate of about twenty percent a year.

Wild horses also overpopulate and overgraze, in the view of people who decline to see the western states as a vacant niche for the feral horse. It is often charged with

The ibex (right), a mountain goat hunted for its horns in its native Siberia, now leaps canyons and cliffs of the Southwest.

An Asian elk often called a deer, the sika thrives in feral herds in Maryland, Virginia, and Texas (opposite). Sikas were first released in 1916 on Maryland's James Island. Some of these able swimmers crossed Chesapeake Bay to the mainland. Others, introduced to Assateague Island, prosper in a herd of about 1,000.

usurping cattle range—as "America's number-one interloper." It has long been treated as a pest. From the early 1900's, mustangers, now outlawed, rounded up horses for the hide buyer, and soon after for chicken-feed and pet-food factories.

Wild horses live in remote, rugged country. They cannot be counted accurately, but in 1925 they were estimated at about 1,000,000. By 1971 the Bureau of Land Management guessed that only about 17,000 ranged public

land in nine western states. Then animal lovers saw the fruition of a nationwide campaign: the Wild Free-Roaming Horse and Burro Act, which promised to halt the slaughter. But it has not solved the problem.

Today more than 50,000 wild horses (and some 10,000 burros) graze western rangelands. But overcrowding has been eased, as has competition with native wildlife and domestic stock, by the federal Adopt-A-Horse program. Since the law was passed in 1976, about 15,000 horses have found new homes with citizens in almost every state.

Into the arid Southwest, one day in 1856, strode 34 camels, brought from the Near East to serve the U. S. Army as pack animals. They turned out to be touchy, independent creatures, biting, kicking, and spitting at the mule skinners who mistreated them. They spooked the cavalry horses and frightened citizens. Even so, more were imported, some by civilians. Eventually the unfortunate camels were sold or turned out to fend for themselves. They wandered the desert, it is said, until 1901, occasionally producing young, and turning up now and then, like phantoms, in a mining camp or a ranch yard.

Not all our exotic species were invited. Most unwelcome are the Old World rats and mice. Native to Asia, all live near humans. As fellow travelers, the house mouse and the black rat had spread to Europe by the Middle Ages. Then in the 16th century they scrambled aboard ships to the New World. They put ashore on America's east coast and soon also on the west.

By 1825 the black rat had become so well established on the east coast that it was taken to be a native mammal. The Norway rat appeared in the American colonies about 1775—the English claimed the colonists had brought it in with smuggled goods, and the colonists blamed the English, while *Rattus norvegicus* went about its own colonizing, covering the continent.

Worldwide, rats and mice eat and contaminate about a fifth of all food crops planted. In the United States alone, in a year's time, they damage or destroy property worth $1 billion. They gnaw wiring and cause innumerable fires. Through fecal droppings, they transmit several diseases to humans. Their parasites carry such diseases as murine typhus and plague—the "black death," which killed an estimated one of every three Europeans between 1347 and 1350. Plague is transmitted by fleas among rats and other small mammals. If its animal host dies, the flea may move to and infect a nearby human.

Rat-borne plague struck San Francisco in 1900 and Los Angeles in 1924. The disease smolders here in such wild animals as prairie dogs, rabbits, and squirrels. An average of 14 people contract plague every year, mostly in the western states.

But the house mouse and the Norway rat atone for some of the sins of their kind: The albino strains of both species are the mice and rats of medical laboratories. And biologists tell us that "dirty rat" is slander, that

Not quite at home on the range, these imported ungulates roam commercial game ranches in Texas. With more than 30 other species native to Africa and Eurasia, axis deer (opposite), oryx (above), and blackbuck antelope (left) lure hunters from all over the world. Sometimes the "Texotics" escape their fences. No one yet knows whether the free-ranging grazers and browsers will adapt to a new habitat in harmony with native species. The Texas game laws do not protect most exotics. In any season a handsome rack can become a trophy on a "no kill, no pay" safari.

laboratory rats quickly rid themselves of parasites, and that rats in the wild groom daily and choose clean food. It is the environment, which we untidy and wasteful humans provide, that makes the rat our enemy.

By far the greatest number of nonnative mammalian species have been brought to North America for the guns of hunters, and often with little forethought. A particularly bad choice was the European rabbit. In spite of its infamous past—this rabbit ravaged Australia in the late 1800's and thousands of miles of fence failed to stop it—it was released in the Midwest in the 1950's for hunting and for running in beagle field trials.

The animals came from the San Juan Islands north of Puget Sound, where they had lived since about 1900, and where their multitudes had eaten plant cover to the ground and burrowed so extensively that the bluffs of one island crumbled into the sea. Luckily the introductions in the 1950's and others later seem to have failed.

In the Great Smoky Mountains they tell about wild "Rooshians," the boars imported there in 1912 to a private game preserve for sporting gentlemen. From Russia—or Germany, depending on who's telling the story—came 14 wild boars, to be penned in a great enclosure so that they could "increase in number." On the first hunt, a few years later, the powerful hogs knocked down the fence and escaped into the woods. Interbreeding with feral domestic swine, they have increased in number ever since.

Up to 2,000 boars now range the Great Smoky Mountains National Park alone. Both inside the park and outside (where they are hunted), their rooting erodes soil, destroys the habitat of small ground-dwelling animals, and, at high elevations, has stripped a large percentage of the plant cover. Park officials woefully point to the boars as another example of the devastation that a nonnative species can wreak in an ecosystem.

But in the Southwest, a wildlife manager justifies the importing of game animals by citing "our American tradition that every citizen should have the right . . . to hunt." Another suggests "limiting the kill to the most admirable and challenging creatures." Some state game commissions have endorsed the careful introduction of exotics to land depleted of native game. Most importations, however, have been made by private landowners, who cite their success in providing sanctuary for some species that are threatened with extinction in their native lands. The exotic-species count today—highest in Texas—is about three dozen.

Ranchers have gone into the game business in a big way. Hunters pay fees to bag exotic trophies—up to $950 for an axis deer or $1,200 for a Barbary sheep. On many ranches, the income from hunting exceeds that from livestock. Usually "Texotics" are fenced. But there is always the chance that a species will establish a wild breeding population and threaten native wildlife.

The European hare was also imported for sport hunting. By the 1920's it had made its mark as a clever quarry—and a pest to farmers. Another small mammal, the nutria, brought from South America to Louisiana as an experiment in breeding a new furbearer, became a major money crop for the trapper.

The haphazard history of the nutria in Louisiana began in 1938. Several pairs were imported from Argentina and placed in "escape-proof" pens at Avery Island. Here they multiplied, prospered—and escaped, many during a 1940 hurricane. More were imported. By the late 1950's Louisiana counted 20,000,000 nutrias nibbling away at its wetland. The pelt supply zoomed. The market slumped. Then in 1957 Hurricane Audrey further destroyed the vegetation cover that the nutrias themselves had damaged, and in one bad winter millions of nutrias froze to death. Their population stabilized, and the native muskrat population declined. Prices for nutria skins rose, and Louisiana had a multimillion-dollar nutria industry. But what happened was all a game of chance. To protect native plants and animals, we must stop taking chances.   STEPHEN R. SEATER

Horse *(Equus caballus)*

Strong legs and the hoof (that single digit upon which the horse runs) give *E. caballus*—agile, fleet, ever on its toes—the most advanced limb structure in the order Perissodactyla. Wild horses roam pockets of British Columbia and the western United States. To most eyes, they are a motley crew, the Spanish blood long ago diluted by feral horses of many breeds. Color varies. An occasional palomino, black, white, or pinto appears among the brown and

bay multitudes. Today's wild horse, while often foraging a meager range, grows to about 5 feet (1.5 m) at the withers.

Though small, wild horses prove their stamina. They can run for miles, spurting to 35 miles an hour. Swift flight is the horse's instinctive first defense, though the natural predators it once faced, such as cougars, are gone from most of its range.

Wild horses often travel in herds of three to 20 animals—but a herd can be larger. A stallion usually commands, with an older mare as

lieutenant. So dominant is a prime stallion that his herd is known as a harem and he furiously fights off any rival. To drive his mares, the harem master lowers his head, stretches his neck, and lays back his ears. Dawdlers get a sharp nip on the flank. When the horses graze or drink at a water hole, the stallion stands guard.

Mares go off on their own to foal. Gestation takes 11 months, and the young usually are born in the spring.

Colts stay with the herd until, at about three years old, they show signs of growing up. Until the age of six or seven, they roam (like the young stallion above) with other bachelors. By raiding or by deposing an old stallion, they get their own harems.

OVERLEAF: *Wild spirits flee, spurred by a dappled stallion as rearguard. When a herd takes flight, a shrewd old mare chooses the escape route.*

Norway Rat (*Rattus norvegicus*)

Black Rat (*Rattus rattus*)

A climber and high-wire artist, using its long, scaly tail as a balancing pole, the black rat seeks lofty places. It colonizes attics and rafters of barns and buildings—thus its other name, roof rat. It seldom descends to burrows, basements, or sewers. Outdoors—in affluent Florida and California neighborhoods, for instance—this "bare-tailed squirrel" nests in trees.

R. *rattus* once disembarked daily at ports in the U. S. and Mexico. Modern ratproof ship construction and inspection methods have virtually blocked that route. It lives along the south Atlantic and Gulf coasts and on the west coast north to British Columbia.

Seldom does the black rat weigh as much as a pound (0.5 kg) or exceed 18 inches (46 cm) overall.

Its slender build, longer tail, and naked, prominent ears distinguish it from the larger Norway rat.

Companion and foe of humans from earliest times, R. *rattus* lives by devouring immeasurable amounts of our food. The settlers at Jamestown, wrote Captain John Smith in 1609, found their supply of cracked corn "so consumed with the many thousand rats, increased first from the ships, that we knewe not how to keepe that little wee had. This did drive us all to our wits ende."

At wit's end is where we often are today, trying to cope with the proliferation of these rodents. Some researchers say that traps and poisons only make room for more. The rats breed year-round, with five or six litters a year and up to seven young per litter. Offspring begin to breed by the fourth month. Mortality among young rats is high, but a pair theoretically could produce 1,500 descendants in a life span of one year.

"The finest . . . product that Nature has managed to create" is probably the Norway rat, wrote naturalist Ivan T. Sanderson. Adaptability—both behavioral and genetic—is perhaps the most distinguishing trait of R. *norvegicus*.

In every state, in Mexico, and in southern and western Canada, wherever people have concentrated, and in rural areas nearby, the Norway rat lives. Although in temperate climates it may summer in grainfield or haystack and winter in barn or silo, this rat prefers human density, with its food waste and diversified shelter. A burrower, it lives on ground floors, in basements, tunnels, garbage dumps, and—since it is also a great swimmer—in sewers.

Of heavier build and with a shorter tail than R. *rattus*, the Norway rat has reddish-gray to brownish-gray fur that gives it another name—the brown rat. In spite of tales exaggerating its size, even the largest weigh less than 2 pounds (0.9 kg).

Norway rats eat almost anything, though they prefer grains, meat, eggs, fruit, or a chance to sort out the garbage. Rats sample all new food cautiously. If bait tastes strange or makes them ill, they will become bait-shy and reject it forever.

They live in hierarchical groups. The dominant males, their females, and offspring nest closest to the food supply. Again and again, the strongest survive to breed most successfully. Their high breeding rate also has allowed the rapid spread of genes that provide resistance to anticoagulant poisons, thus producing a "super rat" which, so far, defies our attempts to eradicate it.

House Mouse (*Mus musculus*)

Anything we eat, *M. musculus* eats. Biologists call such a species a "human commensal," an animal that shares our table—and usually our buildings. But the house mouse also nests in meadows, grainfields, and sand dunes. Any place in North America where people live or visit, it makes its home. Its length, including tail, is from 5.1 to 7.8 inches (130 to 198 mm).

The tiny size of the buff-bellied, gray-brown rodent is, for it, both a curse and a blessing. It is prey to larger meat-eating animals.

But the mouse can hide in the smallest crevice or hole, under any leaf or rock, in cupboards, drawers, and coat pockets.

We often feel affection for this tiny animal—"little mouse" is a term of endearment. In folk belief, a mouse was the form taken by the soul as it escaped from the mouth at death. And mice "sing" in the night, twittering and churring.

Yet we know that this mouse is a destroyer and contaminator of food and water, a vector for some of the diseases carried by the infamous rat, and a pest worthy of pursuit by our folklore farmer's

wife. In cities where poisons and improved sanitation reduce rat populations, the mouse menace increases in proportion. Their food, water, and range needs are limited, and they show greater resistance to anticoagulants.

Like most rodents, *M. musculus* is prolific. Females tend to come into heat in the presence of males and produce from five to 14 litters a year. (The one above

is newborn.) Each litter of three to 12 may breed in six weeks.

House mice colonize. Dominant males establish both a home range, clearly marked by odor (probably urine), and a family of several females and young. Members of foreign groups are attacked and cast out. This ensures some genetic isolation, reinforcing genes adapted to the environment. If a community grows too large, groups of young leave to form new colonies. Thus *M. musculus* exploits genetics and chance in the battle for survival.

Nutria (*Myocastor coypus*)

Its thick fur makes a fashionable jacket worth $1,500 or more. But tunneling in dikes and gobbling in sugarcane fields makes an outlaw of this marsh-loving rodent—the nutria, or coypu, as it is also called. The only member of the family Capromyidae successfully introduced to North America, *M. coypus* lives along streams and rivers of southern Canada and scattered areas of the United States from Maryland to the state of Washington. It flourishes in the warm Gulf Coast climate.

A streamlined swimmer, a nutria has a triangular head, small ears that close out the water as it dives, and webbed hind feet. A female bears one to three litters a year, as many as nine young each time. Fully furred at birth, the young can navigate on their own when only five days old. But they usually stay with the mother six to eight weeks. As she swims, they ride on her back and can nurse in transit—the mammary glands are conveniently high on her sides, above the waterline. Before the young are full-grown they may breed.

An adult is a robust 8 to 20 pounds (3.6 to 9 kg), about 3 feet (91 cm) long, including a round, scaly tail. Nearly hiding the soft, gray underfur are long, coarse guard hairs of yellowish or reddish brown. Originally, the fur trade prized only the underfur of the belly. As fashion changes, the market also uses long-haired pelts, as well as sheared or plucked.

Cattail, sedges, and water weeds are favorite foods of the usually gluttonous nutria. A dense population can strip marsh areas of vegetation, creating a wasteland that Louisianans call an "eat-out." A burrower, the nutria dens in banks of rivers or streams, and can honeycomb a rice-field levee. In shallow water, *M. coypus* mounds reeds and other plants (as above) for grooming and feeding platforms.

European Hare (*Lepus capensis*)

Head over heels on a downhill sprint; a straightaway spurt at 30 miles an hour; an uphill streak on long hind legs—these are the speed feats that make the European hare a challenging game species. (Until recently it was classified as *L. europaeus*.)

These hares—at 25 to 27.5 inches (64 to 70 cm) the largest in their range—occur in Ontario, Canada, and in the northeastern corner of the U. S. They prefer open country where in the daytime they crouch in clumps of grass or brush. At dusk they emerge to feed on grass and herbs in summer, twigs and bark in winter. If discovered by a hawk, fox, bobcat, or a human hunter, they usually bolt, artfully dodging and doubling back on the pursuer. *L. capensis* has been known to lead dogs across ice thick enough for itself but too thin for them, to bound with ease over a five-foot wall, and to swim wide rivers.

The kinky, grizzled pelage, brown in summer (above), lightens in winter. European hares are active year-round, and the first young of the breeding season may appear when snow is on the ground. The doe scatters the leverets among nearby nests. When returning to nurse them, she often utters a faint grunt, which they answer. By March she may be pregnant again.

Wild Boar (*Sus scrofa*)

Signs that the wild boar is near: a wallow in a streambed, earth bulldozed far and wide, tree trunks scraped and muddied.

Member of the Old World family Suidae, this boar—long since interbred with feral domestic swine—ranges marsh, forest, and mountain in New Hampshire, California, and southern states.

Few predators vex this giant among pigs, and only the black bear is its match. Built like a small bison, S. *scrofa* grows about 3 feet (91 cm) tall.

If disturbed, boars usually flee, and they are swift, agile runners. But when antagonized, they fight, slashing with deadly tusks. These elongated canine teeth (right) grow continually, sharpening as they wear against each other. With tusks and a disc-shaped snout of strong cartilage, S. *scrofa* grubs

for roots, tubers, insects, and earthworms. Sharp incisors tear up grasses, crop nuts and fruit, or chomp on snakes—even rattlers—sometimes killed first by a blow from a sharp hoof. Fungi, leaves, snails, young birds, small animals, are all fare for a hungry boar.

Boars usually forage at dawn or dusk, though some are completely nocturnal. Except for breeding, most males travel alone, females and young in small bands.

Cooling off in a mud wallow may consume much of a wild boar's day. Occasionally, S. *scrofa* plucks grass or other vegetation with its mouth, spreads it over a small area, and crawls under it. The cut grass is lifted, interwoven with standing grass—and the burly boar relaxes in the shade of a lacy canopy.

Burro (*Equus asinus*)

"The tattered outlaw of the earth" in G. K. Chesterton's poem, *E. asinus* is many things to many people. The tourist on a Death Valley road sees a cute little moocher. The Grand Canyon backpacker finds a fouler of water holes. A park ranger confronts a competitor of native wildlife. Ass of the Bible, *el burro* of the Spanish padre, pack animal of the gold rush, donkey of children's zoos—it has been these also.

Descended from animals lost or cast off since the 16th century, an estimated 10,000 burros roam southwestern North America. But they are hard to count in their remote canyons, mountains, and deserts. They are hardy animals of all seasons, have no natural predators, and overpopulate much of their range.

The long-eared burro has a shaggy coat—usually brown, gray, or black and often lighter at nose and belly. It has small, sure feet, an erect mane, and a tufted tail.

An average adult weighs about 400 pounds (181 kg) and stands up to 4 feet (1.2 m) at the withers.

A female with young forms the only stable social unit. Jacks may dominate a small territory or wander in changing bachelor groups, breaking off to pursue a jenny in heat (above) or to battle in a melee of brays and hoofs, where the teeth of one male can grip an ear of the other and whirl him in a circle.

The jenny bears a foal—about every year and a half—after a gestation of 12 months. Before it is a week old, the suckling begins to forage with its mother and test its keen nose for water. Whether in alpine meadow or desert wash, burros are not fussy eaters. They crop grasses or shrubs, thriving on plants most browsers reject: A burro can de-spine the prickliest cactus to get the pulp inside.

The Ultimate Mammal

The mammals called people (the species *Homo sapiens*) are the only existing members of the family Hominidae of the order of Primates. Our species seems to have originated in the Eastern Hemisphere about 200,000 years ago and to have entered the Americas at least 20,000 years ago. For most of this time *H. sapiens* seems to have had little effect on other species. But toward the end of the last Ice Age, people attained numbers and cultural levels that allowed intensive hunting of the largest land mammals. About 12,000 years ago, such skilled hunters began moving across North America.

From fossil remains we know that during the next several thousand years there was a wave of extinction unsurpassed since the end of the dinosaurs. Mammoths, horses, ground sloths, giant beavers, and about 30 other kinds of large mammals disappeared from North America. Why? Scientists have offered several theories: Perhaps hunters killed so many plant-eaters that those species died off, and the carnivores, such as the lion and saber-toothed tiger, then perished for lack of prey. Or perhaps hunters merely finished off species already in decline because of deteriorating environments. Or possibly people had only an indirect effect—by disrupting the ecological and behavioral patterns of animals.

Sea mammals were largely unaffected by the catastrophe that engulfed land mammals at the end of the Pleistocene. But by the 15th century, when the second major human invasion of North America began, people had learned how to efficiently hunt sea-dwelling species. And because marine mammals were highly visible and yielded meat, oil, and other products, they were pursued intensively.

Explorers found two species of sirenians at opposite corners of the continent. Meat-hungry Russian sailors wiped out the giant Steller's sea cow by 1768, only 27 years after its discovery in the Bering Sea. The manatee, found in the waters of Florida and adjacent areas, was in trouble soon after. But somehow that species survived until it was protected by state law in 1893. Not so fortunate was its neighbor, the Caribbean monk seal, one of the world's few tropical pinnipeds. Already declining rapidly by 1800, the species lingered in remote areas through the mid-20th century. Recent surveys indicate that the seal is extinct (page 285).

Pinnipeds that do not gather in vast breeding colonies usually have avoided excessive human exploitation. Species that do concentrate periodically in small areas have met disaster. Hunters killed so many Guadalupe fur seals and northern elephant seals along the coast of California and Baja California that both species were thought extinct in the late 19th century. Each seal has since been rediscovered, protected by law, and allowed to increase in numbers.

The northern fur seal was easily slaughtered when some 2,500,000 gathered each year on a few small islands in the Bering Sea. Several times attempts to control the killing created political crises involving Great Britain, Russia, Japan, and the United States. In 1911, when only 200,000 animals remained, these nations agreed to jointly protect the herds. The seal population subsequently increased to about 1,800,000.

One of the most important industries of the New England colonies was whaling. Initial targets included the coastal-ranging Atlantic gray whale, which apparently disappeared in the 1700's, and the right whale. As stocks declined in the 18th century, American whalers turned north after the bowhead whale of arctic waters and spread over the world's seas in pursuit of the sperm whale. By about 1860 whaling had slackened in the United States, but new developments allowed other nations to intensify their whaling.

Perfection of the harpoon gun in the 1860's led to large-scale exploitation of the swift-moving blue, fin, and sei whales. During the early 1900's tremendous stocks of whales were discovered in antarctic waters, and soon these were being hard hit by whalers operating from island bases.

The 1920's saw the first factory ships, which fully processed at sea the carcasses of whales killed by crews in smaller accompanying boats. With this innovation came a substantial increase in the take of the blue whale, the largest animal that has ever lived. After a peak kill of 29,606 in 1931, there was a steady decline to only 613 in the last season before the blue whale was given international protection in 1966. Once there may have been 200,000 blue whales; the maximum current worldwide estimate is about 11,000. Some biologists doubt that the species can survive. The threatened extermination of the blue whale might be viewed as the culmination of a process that began in the Pleistocene: Human hunters, acting solely on the basis of immediate need, have systematically eliminated the large mammals of the earth.

Fortunately, during the 1930's a number of critically threatened species of whales were jointly protected by several nations. The most notable success of these measures was the recovery of gray whales along the west coast of North America. In 1946, the International Whaling Commission, a regulatory body now made up of 23 member nations, was formed. Although the commission has totally protected some species and set quotas on others, its effectiveness has been reduced by lack of cooperation from nations that have continued excessive harvests.

Concern for whales and other sea mammals led to enactment of the United States Marine Mammal Protection Act of 1972. This law basically prohibits the killing of marine mammals. But it allows numerous exceptions. One controversy involves the sea otter. This species was pursued mercilessly by fur hunters in the 18th and 19th centuries. Barely 2,000 remained in 1911 when international protection was established. Today about 120,000 live in Alaskan waters alone. There, and in California, sea otters are being accused of depleting fisheries. Some people consider a harvest of them practical.

Valuable furbearing mammals have played an important role in human history. The search for pelts drew Russian adventurers across Siberia and into Alaska during the 1700's. Earlier, French explorers had penetrated the heart of North America and started to establish fur-trade routes. With the same objective, the English chartered the Hudson's Bay Company in 1670. Much of the Anglo-French rivalry on the continent over the next century resulted from competition for the fur trade. After the United States gained independence, the lure of furs stimulated westward movement.

As beavers became scarce in the West by the 1860's, trappers began to concentrate on the central plains. In such open habitat, they used not traps but poison to take wolves and other carnivorous furbearers. Early in the 20th century some eastern lowlands were discovered to be rich in furs. Surprisingly, the leading fur-producing area of the entire continent became—and continues to be—the state of Louisiana. The industry there was built primarily around the muskrat populations in the vast coastal marshes, but by 1962 the nutria, a rodent introduced from South America, was yielding greater profits.

Historically, the fur trade has depended upon such variables as economic conditions, fashions, and the population levels of target mammals. By the 1900's, trapping and habitat disruption had eliminated the beaver, marten, and fisher over most of the eastern United States. The river otter had been exterminated in many areas. Small furbearers, such as the mink, seemed destined to disappear in some states. Indeed, the sea mink of New England already had been eradicated.

Eskimos with flensing tools slice a bowhead whale to ribbons at Barrow, Alaska. Though endangered, the species may be legally hunted by aboriginal Americans. They follow ancestral ways as they communally harvest the whale. But to kill it they lay aside their ivory-tipped harpoons and pick up their guns.

In the 1930's and the 1940's, history began to favor the fur trade's targets. Conservationists had won regulations putting many furbearers and their habitats under some kind of protection. The Depression and World War II slackened demand for luxurious furs. Most furbearers managed to maintain themselves or even make moderate recoveries. The most spectacular comeback has been the beaver's. It has reoccupied or has been reintroduced into much of its former range.

Some conservationists are still concerned about the impact of fur trapping, especially on mammals not covered by detailed regulations. In recent years there has been a general rise in prices for pelts, and a correspondingly greater kill of some species.

An increased harvest of bobcat fur came on top of large kills for sport and predator control—even though there were authoritative reports of seriously declining populations. Since most bobcat pelts were sold abroad, the United States Government began to impose restrictions under an international trade convention that currently involves 54 nations. This agreement attempts to control commerce in many kinds of endangered wildlife, including all species of cats. Some states have improved research and management programs dedicated to the bobcat. But the controversy remains: How much protection does the bobcat need?

Furbearers are not the only animals preyed upon by the ultimate mammal. Hunters for the skin trade killed untold numbers of deer and bison. Indeed, the production of buffalo robes was a major industry during the 19th century. Large mammals were also hunted in great numbers for food and for sport as the frontier advanced. In the 16th century, the bison may have numbered 60,000,000, inhabiting not only the Great Plains but also the East as far as New York and Florida. By the 1830's the bison had been exterminated east of the Mississippi. By 1890 barely 1,000 survived, mostly in Canada. Subsequent conservation efforts sometimes are hailed as having saved the species. But in terms of the

continent-wide ecological role it once played, the bison may be gone forever.

Declines of other big-game mammals in North America were nearly as catastrophic. The pronghorn, once almost as abundant as the bison, suffered a comparable fate as the plains were settled in the 19th century. Even before the American Revolution, the white-tailed deer had become so rare in the East that some colonies enacted protective laws. By 1900 there was fear for the survival of

example, the number of pronghorns in the United States was estimated at 26,000; today the estimate is 500,000. In the same period, white-tailed deer are believed to have increased from 500,000 to 12,450,000. What were described as mere "scattered herds" of mule deer now is an estimated population of 2,250,000. The elk's comeback has been estimated to be from 41,000 in 1900 to nearly 1,000,000 today. Moose, nearly wiped out in 1900, now are up to about 12,000 in the lower

Locked moose antlers, remnant of a deadly duel, provide a red fox with a calcium-rich snack. Small mammals often feed on discarded antlers, for nothing is wasted in the food web of a natural environment. Here at Isle Royale National Park, natural controls still govern. Wolves cull moose, helping to keep the herd at a level the island can support.

both that species and the related mule deer of the West. By the same time elk had disappeared in the eastern, central, and southwestern United States, and moose survived only in a few remote northern areas.

State laws and management programs, supported by federal funds and habitat protection, have reversed the disastrous trends of the previous century. Most of the big-game species have been restored to substantial portions of their historic ranges. In 1900, for

48 states. There are at least another 130,000 moose in Alaska and 600,000 in Canada.

In much of the West, though, mule deer again are declining, partly because of habitat manipulation by people. In some areas, elk are threatened by oil exploration, agriculture, and logging. Yet, around the Great Lakes, white-tailed deer appear to have suffered because there is no longer enough logging to create favorable open habitat. Bighorn sheep and caribou seem more vulnerable to human interference than do most other big-game species and do not respond as well to conservation efforts. Although some populations reportedly are thriving, there are fewer bighorns in the United States now than there were in the 1920's. For most of the last hundred years there has been a general downward trend in caribou numbers in Alaska and Canada. And the future of that species is clouded by the increasing tempo of oil and gas exploitation in the Arctic.

Killing for subsistence, sport, or profit—even when excessive—seldom involves dislike of the target mammals. But strong hatred flares in the warfare against carnivorous mammals that threaten livestock.

Colonial governments authorized bounty payments to persons killing wolves, bears, cougars, and other predators. The pattern repeated itself as the frontier advanced. The bounty system, however, not only was wasteful and destructive but also sometimes failed entirely. Small predators often bred fast enough to withstand the pressure. Large species usually collapsed only when the wilderness was broken up and their ranges became accessible to people.

Human extermination of deer and other natural prey species probably contributed to the decline of carnivores and may have stimulated their depredation on domestic animals. By the early 20th century, the cougar and gray wolf had been exterminated in the eastern United States, except for a few remote forests. The aggressive grizzly bear, always restricted to the West, was then rare in most stock-raising areas. The black bear, less obnoxious to people and more able to adapt to their presence, survived over much of the East, as well as in most of the West.

The United States Government began its own predator-control campaign in 1915. The killing was fostered by pressure from the livestock industry and concern about the predatory mammals that still inhabited the newly formed national forests of the West. The gray wolf was the first major target, and by 1930 that species was practically a thing of the past in the West. Government wolf-control measures later were extended to Alaska, and emulated by Canada, mainly to protect caribou and introduced reindeer herds.

The most consistently and heavily hunted predator of this century has been the coyote. The federal kill often exceeded 100,000 per year. Far more have been killed by farmers, state and local agents, bounty hunters, sportsmen, and trappers. The spreading of poison bait was long a favorite means of killing coyotes and other predators. Conservationists fighting that method argued that many non-target species were being decimated by indiscriminate poisoning. Finally, a 1972 presidential order banned the general use of poison for predator control.

Are too many cougars being killed to protect livestock in the Southwest? Should wolf numbers be controlled to increase numbers of caribou in Alaska and deer in southeastern Canada? Can the grizzly populations of the Yellowstone region and western Montana—the last in the lower 48 states—be maintained in the face of increasing commercial development and recreational activity? Perhaps all such questions boil down to this: Is there room for more than one large meat-eating mammal on the continent?

Large carnivores have not been the only mammals labeled as public enemies. Official poisoning operations have been directed against meadow voles that damaged fruit trees, muskrats that burrowed into dikes, porcupines that destroyed timber—and a host of other rodents. The most widespread campaigns have been aimed at eradicating ground squirrels and prairie dogs because they allegedly fed on crops and pasture.

The reduction of prairie dog numbers on the Great Plains apparently has caused the near-extinction of a species dependent upon them for prey—the black-footed ferret. Such indirect impacts, now increasing through growth of human population and technology, constitute the most serious problems facing American wildlife. Environmental disruption may hurt nearly all mammals, but the most susceptible are small species, which have strict limits on their habitats or food supplies.

Great Gull Island, off Long Island, New York, once had its own species of vole. During the Spanish-American War, amid fears that the East Coast would be attacked, fortifications were built on the island. The vole's tiny habitat was obliterated, and the species has not been seen since.

During the winter of 1972-1973, specimens that resembled the widespread marsh rice rat *Oryzomys palustris*—but with a unique silvery pelage—were found on Cudjoe Key at the southern tip of Florida. In the November 1978 *Journal of Mammalogy* the rodent was formally named *Oryzomys argentatus*—the silver rice rat—and it thus became the newest recognized species of mammal in North America. The entire species seems to be restricted to a freshwater cattail marsh of less than five acres. Comparable places in the Florida Keys have been largely destroyed for mosquito control and housing development. The same situation now confronts the silver rice rat. And so our newest mammal is already among our most endangered. Many other species of rodents, insectivores, and bats are jeopardized in Florida and other rapidly developing parts of the Sun Belt.

Should we worry that these small creatures may pass from the scene? Is not extinction a normal process that will overtake them anyway? When people occupy an area and use it to their advantage are they not acting the same as any other mammal?

Extinction is a natural process. So is the death of an individual. But this does not mean murder should be condoned. People have the ability not only to modify the environment but also to find and implement means of conservation. While we may never again have room for great herds of wild bison, we can preserve all the habitat required by dozens of smaller species. We therefore can insure that at least some of our native mammals, living as they should, under fully natural ecological and behavioral conditions, will remain with us.   RONALD M. NOWAK

Research biologist David Mech approaches his subject with a syringe on a stick. A wolf is first caught in a foot trap. Then, after an injection of a tranquilizer takes effect, the wolf is fitted with a collar containing a radio for tracking the animal's movements. Mech (an author in this book) then carries the wolf to a secluded spot for recovery. Such studies lead to better protection for this vanishing species.

OVERLEAF: *Regally silhouetted in Yellowstone National Park, a lordly moose wades gilded shallows. Once nearly gone from the United States, the moose now gets protection from the ultimate mammal.*

Mammals of the Nearctic Realm

These are the native species of mammals found as far south as Mexico City. Not included are species whose ranges, while extending north of Mexico City, are mainly in tropical areas near the Mexican coasts. General ranges are given for species not described in the order chapters. (C S N W E are symbols for central, southern, northern, western, and eastern respectively.) Species described in this book are indicated by an asterisk. The mammals are listed here in taxonomic sequence. Elsewhere in the book, however, the sequence is sometimes changed to allow for better display of identifying illustrations.

Order Marsupialia Marsupials

Family Didelphidae
New World Opossums

Didelphis virginiana, Virginia Opossum

Order Insectivora Insectivores

Family Soricidae
Shrews

Sorex cinereus, Masked Shrew: Can., N U. S.
S. hydrodromus, Pribilof Shrew: St. Paul Island, Alas.
S. lyelli, Mt. Lyell Shrew: C Calif.
S. preblei, Preble's Shrew: Ore. to Mont.
S. milleri, Carmen Mountain Shrew: NE Mex.
S. longirostris, Southeastern Shrew: SE U. S.
S. vagrans, Vagrant Shrew: W N.A., Alas. to C Mex.
S. ornatus, Ornate Shrew: Calif., N Baja Calif.
S. tenellus, Inyo Shrew: E Calif., SW Nev.
S. trigonirostris, Ashland Shrew: SW Ore.
S. nanus, Dwarf Shrew: Mont. to New Mex.
S. juncensis, Tule Shrew: N Baja Calif.
S. sinuosus, Suisun Shrew: Calif.
S. macrodon, Large-toothed Shrew: E Mex.
S. palustris, Water Shrew
S. alaskanus, Glacier Bay Water Shrew: Alas.
S. bendirii, Pacific Water Shrew: SW Brit. Col. to NW Calif.
S. fumeus, Smoky Shrew: SE Can., NE U. S.
S. arcticus, Arctic Shrew: Can., Alas., NC U. S.
S. gaspensis, Gaspé Shrew: SE Quebec, N New Bruns.
S. dispar, Long-tailed or Rock Shrew: Maine to North Car.
S. trowbridgii, Trowbridge's Shrew: SW Brit. Col. to C Calif.
S. merriami, Merriam's Shrew: W U. S.
S. saussurei, Saussure's Shrew: C Mex. to Guatemala
S. oreopolus, Mexican Long-tailed Shrew: C Mex.
Microsorex hoyi, Pygmy Shrew
Blarina brevicauda, Short-tailed Shrew
B. carolinensis, Southern Short-tailed Shrew

B. telmalestes, Swamp Short-tailed Shrew: SE Va., NE North Car.
Cryptotis parva, Least Shrew: E and C U. S., NE Mex. to Panama
C. mexicana, Mexican Small-eared Shrew: C Mex.
C. goldmani, Goldman's Small-eared Shrew: C Mex. to Guatemala
Notiosorex crawfordi, Desert Shrew

Family Talpidae
Moles

Neurotrichus gibbsii, Shrew-mole: SW Brit. Col. to C Calif.
Scapanus townsendii, Townsend's Mole: SW Brit. Col. to NW Calif.
S. orarius, Coast Mole: SW Brit. Col. to W Idaho and NW Calif.
S. latimanus, Broad-footed Mole: C Ore. to N Baja Calif.
Parascalops breweri, Hairy-tailed Mole
Scalopus aquaticus, Eastern Mole
Condylura cristata, Star-nosed Mole

Order Chiroptera Bats

Family Mormoopidae
Mormoopid Bats

Mormoops megalophylla, Leaf-chinned or Ghost-faced Bat

Family Phyllostomatidae
American Leaf-nosed Bats

Macrotus californicus, California Leaf-nosed Bat
Choeronycteris mexicana, Hog-nosed or Long-tongued Bat
Leptonycteris nivalis, Mexican Long-nosed Bat: SW Tex. to Guatemala
L. sanborni, Sanborn's Long-nosed Bat
Artibeus hirsutus, Hairy Fruit-eating Bat
A. aztecus, Highland Fruit-eating Bat: C Mex. to Panama
Desmodus rotundus, Common Vampire Bat
Diphylla ecaudata, Hairy-legged Vampire Bat: N Mex. to S.A.

Family Natalidae
Funnel-eared Bats

Natalus stramineus, Greater Funnel-eared Bat

Family Vespertilionidae
Vespertilionid Bats

Myotis lucifugus, Little Brown Myotis
M. yumanensis, Yuma Myotis: Brit. Col. to C Mex.
M. austroriparius, Southeastern Myotis: SE U. S.
M. grisescens, Gray Myotis
M. velifer, Cave Myotis: SW U. S. to Honduras
M. keenii, Keen's Myotis
M. evotis, Long-eared Myotis: SW Can., W U. S., Baja Calif.

M. milleri, Miller's Myotis: N Baja Calif.
M. auriculus, Southwestern Myotis: SW U. S., N Mex.
M. thysanodes, Fringed Myotis: S Brit. Col. to S Mex.
M. sodalis, Indiana or Social Myotis: E U. S.
M. volans, Long-legged Myotis: Brit. Col. to C Mex.
M. californicus, California Myotis: Brit. Col. to S Mex.
M. leibii, Small-footed Myotis: S Can. to N Mex.
M. planiceps, Flat-headed Myotis: NE Mex.
Pizonyx vivesi, Mexican Fishing Bat or Fish-eating Bat
Lasionycteris noctivagans, Silver-haired Bat
Pipistrellus hesperus, Western Pipistrelle: S Wash. to C Mex.
P. subflavus, Eastern Pipistrelle
Eptesicus fuscus, Big Brown Bat
Lasiurus borealis, Red Bat
L. seminolus, Seminole Bat: SE U. S.
L. cinereus, Hoary Bat
L. intermedius, Northern Yellow Bat: E U. S., Mex., Cuba
L. ega, Southern Yellow Bat: SW U. S. to S.A.
Nycticeius humeralis, Evening Bat: E U. S., NE Mex.
Rhogeessa alleni, Allen's Yellow Bat: C Mex.
Euderma maculatum, Spotted Bat
Plecotus mexicanus, Mexican Big-eared Bat: Mex.
P. townsendii, Townsend's Big-eared Bat: S Brit. Col. to S Mex.; parts of E U. S.
P. rafinesquii, Rafinesque's Big-eared Bat
Idionycteris phyllotis, Allen's Big-eared Bat: S Utah to C Mex.
Antrozous pallidus, Pallid Bat

Family Molossidae
Free-tailed Bats

Tadarida brasiliensis, Mexican or Brazilian Free-tailed Bat
T. femorosacca, Pocketed Free-tailed Bat: SW U. S., N Mex.
T. macrotis, Big Free-tailed Bat: SW U. S., Mex., West Indies
Eumops perotis, Western Mastiff Bat
E. underwoodi, Underwood's Mastiff Bat: S Ariz. to Honduras
E. glaucinus, Wagner's Mastiff Bat: Fla., West Indies, S Mex. to S.A.

Order Edentata Edentates

Family Dasypodidae
Armadillos

*Dasypus novemcinctus, Common Long-nosed or Nine-banded Armadillo

Order Lagomorpha Lagomorphs

Family Ochotonidae
Pikas

*Ochotona princeps, Pika

Family Leporidae
Hares and Rabbits

Romerolagus diazi, Volcano Rabbit: C Mex.
*Sylvilagus idahoensis, Pygmy Rabbit
S. bachmani, Brush Rabbit: W Ore. to Baja Calif.
*S. palustris, Marsh Rabbit
*S. floridanus, Eastern Cottontail
*S. transitionalis, New England Cottontail
*S. nuttallii, Nuttall's or Mountain Cottontail
*S. audubonii, Desert Cottontail
*S. aquaticus, Swamp Rabbit
*Lepus americanus, Snowshoe Hare
*L. othus, Alaskan Hare
*L. arcticus, Arctic Hare
*L. townsendii, White-tailed Jackrabbit
*L. californicus, Black-tailed Jackrabbit
L. callotis, White-sided Jackrabbit: SW New Mex. to C Mex.
*L. alleni, Antelope Jackrabbit

Order Rodentia Rodents

Family Aplodontidae
Mountain Beaver

*Aplodontia rufa, Mountain Beaver

Family Sciuridae
Squirrels

*Tamias striatus, Eastern Chipmunk
Eutamias alpinus, Alpine Chipmunk: C Calif.
*E. minimus, Least Chipmunk
*E. amoenus, Yellow-pine Chipmunk
*E. townsendii, Townsend's Chipmunk
E. ochrogenys, Yellow-cheeked Chipmunk: NW Calif.
E. senex, Allen's Chipmunk: C Ore., N Calif.
E. siskiyou, Siskiyou Chipmunk: SW Ore., NW Calif.

E. sonomae, Sonoma Chipmunk: NW Calif.
*E. merriami, Merriam's Chipmunk
E. obscurus, Baja California Chipmunk: S Calif., Baja Calif.
*E. dorsalis, Cliff Chipmunk
*E. quadrivittatus, Colorado Chipmunk
E. ruficaudus, Red-tailed Chipmunk: SW Can., NW U. S.
*E. cinereicollis, Gray-collared Chipmunk
E. canipes, Gray-footed Chipmunk: SC New Mex., SW Tex.
E. quadrimaculatus, Long-eared Chipmunk: E Calif., W Nev.
E. speciosus, Lodgepole Chipmunk: Calif., W Nev.
E. panamintinus, Panamint Chipmunk: SE Calif., SW Nev.
E. umbrinus, Uinta Chipmunk: Wyo. to SE Calif.
E. palmeri, Palmer's Chipmunk: S Nev.
E. bulleri, Buller's Chipmunk: N Mex.
*Marmota monax, Woodchuck
*M. flaviventris, Yellow-bellied Marmot
*M. caligata, Hoary Marmot
*M. olympus, Olympic Marmot
M. vancouverensis, Vancouver Marmot: Vancouver Island, Brit. Col.
Ammospermophilus harrisii, Harris' Antelope Squirrel: SW U. S., NW Mex.
*A. leucurus, White-tailed Antelope Squirrel
*A. interpres, Texas Antelope Squirrel
A. nelsoni, Nelson's Antelope Squirrel: C Calif.
Spermophilus townsendii, Townsend's Ground Squirrel: S Wash. to S Nev.
S. washingtoni, Washington Ground Squirrel: SE Wash., NE Ore.
S. brunneus, Idaho Ground Squirrel: SW Idaho
*S. richardsonii, Richardson's Ground Squirrel
*S. armatus, Uinta Ground Squirrel
S. beldingi, Belding's Ground Squirrel: E Ore. to NW Utah and E Calif.
S. columbianus, Columbian Ground Squirrel: SW Can., NW U. S.
*S. parryii, Arctic Ground Squirrel
*S. tridecemlineatus, Thirteen-lined Ground Squirrel

S. mexicanus, Mexican Ground Squirrel: N Tex. to C Mex.
S. spilosoma, Spotted Ground Squirrel: South Dak. to N Mex.
S. perotensis, Perote Ground Squirrel: C Mex.
S. franklinii, Franklin's Ground Squirrel: Alberta to Ind.
*S. variegatus, Rock Squirrel
*S. beecheyi, California Ground Squirrel
S. atricapillus, Baja California Rock Squirrel: Baja Calif.
S. mohavensis, Mohave Ground Squirrel: S Calif.
S. tereticaudus, Round-tailed Ground Squirrel: SW U. S., NW Mex.
*S. lateralis, Golden-mantled Ground Squirrel
S. saturatus, Cascade Golden-mantled Ground Squirrel: SW Brit. Col., C Wash.
S. madrensis, Sierra Madre Mantled Ground Squirrel: NW Mex.
*Cynomys ludovicianus, Black-tailed Prairie Dog
C. mexicanus, Mexican Prairie Dog: NE Mex.
*C. leucurus, White-tailed Prairie Dog
C. parvidens, Utah Prairie Dog: S Utah
C. gunnisoni, Gunnison's Prairie Dog: SW U. S.
*Sciurus carolinensis, Gray Squirrel
S. aureogaster, Mexican Gray Squirrel: Mex.
S. colliaei, Collie's Squirrel: W Mex.
*S. griseus, Western Gray Squirrel
*S. aberti, Abert's Squirrel
*S. niger, Fox Squirrel
S. oculatus, Peters' Squirrel: C Mex.
S. alleni, Allen's Squirrel: NE Mex.
S. nayaritensis, Nayarit Squirrel: SE Ariz., W Mex.
S. arizonensis, Arizona Gray Squirrel: Ariz., W New Mex., NW Mex.
*Tamiasciurus hudsonicus, Red Squirrel
*T. douglasii, Douglas' Squirrel
*Glaucomys volans, Southern Flying Squirrel
*G. sabrinus, Northern Flying Squirrel

Family Geomyidae
Pocket Gophers

Thomomys umbrinus, Southern Pocket Gopher: W U. S., Mex.
T. talpoides, Northern Pocket Gopher: SW Can., W U. S.
*T. mazama, Western Pocket Gopher
T. monticola, Mountain Pocket Gopher: NE Calif., W Nev.
T. bulbivorus, Camas Pocket Gopher: NW Ore.
Zygogeomys trichopus, Michoacán Pocket Gopher: C Mex.
Geomys bursarius, Plains Pocket Gopher: S Manitoba to S Tex.
G. arenarius, Desert Pocket Gopher: S New Mex., W Tex., NE Mex.

G. personatus, Texas Pocket Gopher: S Tex., NE Mex.
G. pinetis, Southeastern Pocket Gopher: S Ala., S Ga., N Fla.
G. colonus, Colonial Pocket Gopher: SE Ga.
G. fontanelus, Sherman's Pocket Gopher: SE Ga.
G. cumberlandius, Cumberland Island Pocket Gopher: SE Ga.
Pappogeomys bulleri, Buller's Pocket Gopher: W Mex.
P. alcorni, Alcorn's Pocket Gopher: W Mex.
P. castanops, Yellow-faced Pocket Gopher: SW Kan. to C Mex.
P. merriami, Merriam's Pocket Gopher: C Mex.
P. neglectus, Querétaro Pocket Gopher: C Mex.
P. fumosus, Smoky Pocket Gopher: C Mex.
P. tylorhinus, Taylor's Pocket Gopher: C Mex.
P. zinseri, Zinser's Pocket Gopher: C Mex.
P. gymnurus, Llano Pocket Gopher: C Mex.

Family Heteromyidae
Heteromyids

Perognathus fasciatus, Olive-backed Pocket Mouse: S Sask. to C Colo.
*P. flavescens, Plains Pocket Mouse
P. parvus, Great Basin Pocket Mouse: S Brit. Col. to N Ariz.
P. alticola, White-eared Pocket Mouse: S Calif.
P. xanthonotus, Yellow-eared Pocket Mouse: S Calif.
*P. flavus, Silky Pocket Mouse
P. longimembris, Little Pocket Mouse: SE Ore. to NW Mex.
P. ampulus, Arizona Pocket Mouse: Ariz., NW Mex.
P. inornatus, San Joaquin Pocket Mouse: C Calif.
P. formosus, Long-tailed Pocket Mouse: SW U. S., Baja Calif.
P. baileyi, Bailey's Pocket Mouse: SW U. S., N Mex.
P. hispidus, Hispid Pocket Mouse: North Dak. to C Mex.
P. penicillatus, Desert Pocket Mouse: SW U. S., N Mex.
P. arenarius, Little Desert Pocket Mouse: Baja Calif.
P. pernix, Sinaloan Pocket Mouse: NW Mex.

Family Heteromyidae
(continued)

P. intermedius, Rock Pocket Mouse:
SW U. S., NW Mex.

P. nelsoni, Nelson's Pocket Mouse:
SE New Mex., W Tex., N Mex.

P. goldmani, Goldman's Pocket Mouse:
NW Mex.

P. artus, Narrow-skulled Pocket
Mouse: NW Mex.

P. lineatus, Lined Pocket Mouse:
C Mex.

P. fallax, San Diego Pocket Mouse:
S Calif., Baja Calif.

P. anthonyi, Anthony's Pocket Mouse:
Cerros Island, NW Baja Calif.

P. californicus, California Pocket
Mouse: Calif., N Baja Calif.

P. spinatus, Spiny Pocket Mouse:
S Calif., Baja Calif.

*Microdipodops megacephalus, Dark
Kangaroo Mouse

*M. pallidus, Pale Kangaroo Mouse

*Dipodomys ordii, Ord's Kangaroo Rat

D. microps, Chisel-toothed Kangaroo
Rat: Ore. to N Ariz.

D. elephantinus, Big-eared Kangaroo
Rat: C Calif.

D. venustus, Narrow-faced Kangaroo
Rat: W Calif.

D. agilis, Agile Kangaroo Rat:
SW Calif., Baja Calif.

D. heermanni, Heermann's Kangaroo
Rat: S Ore., Calif.

D. ingens, Giant Kangaroo Rat:
SW Calif.

D. panamintinus, Panamint Kangaroo
Rat: W Nev., S Calif.

D. stephensi, Stephens' Kangaroo Rat:
SW Calif.

D. gravipes, San Quintín Kangaroo
Rat: NW Baja Calif.

*D. spectabilis, Banner-tailed Kangaroo
Rat

D. nelsoni, Nelson's Kangaroo Rat:
N Mex.

D. elator, Texas Kangaroo Rat:
SW Okla., NC Tex.

D. deserti, Desert Kangaroo Rat:
NW Nev. to NW Mex.

D. phillipsii, Phillips' Kangaroo Rat:
C Mex.

*D. merriami, Merriam's Kangaroo Rat

D. nitratoides, Fresno Kangaroo Rat:
C Calif.

Liomys pictus, Painted Spiny Pocket
Mouse: W and S Mex.

*L. irroratus, Mexican Spiny Pocket
Mouse

Family Castoridae
Beavers

*Castor canadensis, Beaver

Family Cricetidae
New World Rats and Mice

*Oryzomys palustris, Marsh Rice Rat

O. argentatus, Silver Rice Rat:
Cudjoe Key, S Fla.

Reithrodontomys montanus, Plains
Harvest Mouse: South Dak. to NW Mex.

R. burti, Sonoran Harvest Mouse:
NW Mex.

*R. humulis, Eastern Harvest Mouse

R. megalotis, Western Harvest Mouse:
SW Can. to Ind. and C Mex.

*R. raviventris, Salt Marsh Harvest
Mouse

R. chrysopsis, Volcano Harvest Mouse:
C Mex.

R. sumichrasti, Sumichrast's Harvest
Mouse: C Mex. to Panama

R. fulvescens, Fulvous Harvest Mouse:
Mo. to Nicaragua

R. hirsutus, Hairy Harvest Mouse:
C Mex.

R. mexicanus, Mexican Harvest Mouse:
NE Mex. to Costa Rica

*Peromyscus eremicus, Cactus Mouse

P. eva, Eva's Desert Mouse:
S Baja Calif.

P. collatus, Turner Island Canyon
Mouse: Turner Island, NE Mex.

P. guardia, Angel Island Mouse:
islands in Gulf of Calif.

P. hooperi, Hooper's Mouse: NE Mex.

P. merriami, Merriam's Mouse:
S Ariz., NW Mex.

P. californicus, California Mouse:
Calif., N Baja Calif.

*P. maniculatus, Deer Mouse

P. sitkensis, Sitka Mouse: SE Alas.

*P. polionotus, Oldfield Mouse

P. melanotis, Black-eared Mouse: Mex.

*P. leucopus, White-footed Mouse

P. gossypinus, Cotton Mouse: SE U. S.

P. crinitus, Canyon Mouse:
W U. S., NW Mex.

P. boylii, Brush Mouse: SW U. S. to
Honduras

P. attwateri, Texas Mouse: SC U. S.

P. pectoralis, White-ankled Mouse:
S Okla. to C Mex.

P. polius, Chihuahuan Mouse: N Mex.

P. stephani, San Esteban Island Mouse:
San Esteban Island, E Baja, Calif.

P. hylocetes, Southern Wood Mouse:
C Mex.

P. truei, Piñon Mouse: C Ore. to S Mex.

P. difficilis, Rock Mouse:
Col. to C Mex.

P. melanophrys, Plateau Mouse: Mex.

P. ochraventer, El Carrizo Deer Mouse:
C Mex.

P. furvus, Blackish Deer Mouse:
C Mex.

P. simulatus, Jico Deer Mouse: C Mex.

P. floridanus, Florida Mouse: Fla.

*Ochrotomys nuttalli, Golden Mouse

*Baiomys taylori, Pygmy Mouse

Onychomys leucogaster, Northern
Grasshopper Mouse: SC Can., W U. S.,
N Mex.

*O. torridus, Southern Grasshopper
Mouse

*Sigmodon hispidus, Hispid Cotton Rat

S. mascotensis, Jaliscan Cotton Rat:
C Mex.

S. arizonae, Arizona Cotton Rat:
SE Calif., Ariz., NW Mex.

S. fulviventer, Tawny-bellied Cotton
Rat: SE Ariz., W New Mex., N Mex.

S. alleni, Allen's Cotton Rat: W Mex.

S. leucotis, White-eared Cotton Rat:
Mex.

S. ochrognathus, Yellow-nosed Cotton
Rat: SW U. S., N Mex.

Neotomodon alstoni, Volcano Mouse:
C Mex.

*Neotoma floridana, Eastern Woodrat

N. micropus, Southern Plains Woodrat:
SW Kan. to NE Mex.

*N. albigula, White-throated Woodrat

N. nelsoni, Nelson's Woodrat: E Mex.

N. palatina, Bolaños Woodrat:
C Mex.

N. varia, Turner Island Woodrat:
Turner Island, NW Mex.

N. lepida, Desert Woodrat:
SE Ore. to Baja Calif.

N. bryanti, Bryant's Woodrat:
Cerros Island, NW Baja Calif.

N. anthonyi, Anthony's Woodrat:
Todos Santos Island, NW Baja Calif.

N. martinensis, San Martín Island
Woodrat: San Martín Island, NW Baja
Calif.

N. stephensi, Stephen's Woodrat:
SW U. S.

N. goldmani, Goldman's Woodrat:
N Mex.

N. mexicana, Mexican Woodrat:
SW U. S. to Honduras

N. angustapalata, Tamaulipan Woodrat: NE Mex.

N. fuscipes, Dusky-footed Woodrat:
W Ore. to N Baja Calif.

*N. cinerea, Bushy-tailed Woodrat

Nelsonia neotomodon, Diminutive
Woodrat: C Mex.

Clethrionomys rutilus, Northern Red-
backed Vole: Alas., NW Can.

*C. gapperi, Southern Red-backed Vole

C. californicus, California Red-backed
Vole: W Ore., N Calif.

Phenacomys intermedius, Heather
Vole: Can., W U. S.

P. albipes, White-footed Vole:
W Ore., NW Calif.

*P. longicaudus, Red Tree Vole

*Microtus pennsylvanicus, Meadow Vole

M. breweri, Beach Vole:
Muskeget Island, Mass.

M. nesophilus, Gull Island Vole: Great
Gull Island, N.Y. [EXTINCT]

M. montanus, Montane Vole:
SW Can., W U. S.

M. canicaudus, Gray-tailed Vole:
SW Wash., W Ore.

M. californicus, California Vole:
SW Ore. to N Baja Calif.

M. townsendii, Townsend's Vole:
SW Brit. Col. to NW Calif.

M. oeconomus, Tundra Vole:
Alas., NW Can., Eurasia

M. longicaudus, Long-tailed Vole:
E Alas. to New Mex.

M. coronarius, Coronation Island Vole:
SE Alas.

M. mexicanus, Mexican Vole:
SW U. S., Mex.

M. chrotorrhinus, Rock Vole:
SE Can., NE U. S.

*M. xanthognathus, Yellow-cheeked
Vole

M. oregoni, Creeping Vole:
SW Brit. Col. to NW Calif.

M. abbreviatus, Insular Vole: Hall and
St. Matthew islands, Alas.

*M. ochrogaster, Prairie Vole

*M. pinetorum, Woodland Vole

M. quasiater, Jalapan Pine Vole:
C Mex.

M. miurus, Singing Vole:
Alas., NW Can.

M. richardsoni, Water Vole:
SW Can., NW U. S.

Lagurus curtatus, Sagebrush Vole:
SW Can., W U. S.

Neofiber alleni, Round-tailed Muskrat:
S Ga., Fla.

*Ondatra zibethicus, Muskrat

*Lemmus sibiricus, Brown Lemming

*Synaptomys cooperi, Southern Bog
Lemming

*S. borealis, Northern Bog Lemming

*Dicrostonyx groenlandicus, Collared
Lemming

D. exsul, St. Lawrence Island Collared Lemming: Alas.
D. hudsonius, Labrador Collared Lemming: NE Can.

Family Zapodidae
Jumping Mice

*Zapus hudsonius, Meadow Jumping Mouse
Z. princeps, Western Jumping Mouse: SW Can., SE Alas., W U. S.
Z. trinotatus, Pacific Jumping Mouse: SW Brit. Col. to NW Calif.
Napaeozapus insignis, Woodland Jumping Mouse: SE Can., NE U. S.

Family Erethizontidae
New World Porcupines

*Erethizon dorsatum, Porcupine

Order Cetacea Cetaceans

Family Ziphiidae
Beaked Whales

*Berardius bairdii, Baird's Beaked Whale
Mesoplodon bidens, North Atlantic Beaked Whale: Atlantic coast
M. densirostris, Tropical Beaked Whale: Atlantic coast
M. europaeus, Gervais' Beaked Whale: Atlantic coast
M. mirus, True's Beaked Whale: Atlantic coast
M. stejnegeri, North Pacific Beaked Whale: Pacific coast
M. carlhubbsi, Moore's Beaked Whale: Pacific coast
M. ginkgodens, Japanese Beaked Whale: Pacific coast
Ziphius cavirostris, Goose-beaked Whale: Atlantic and Pacific coasts
Hyperoodon ampullatus, Northern Bottlenose Whale: Atlantic coast

Family Physeteridae
Sperm Whales

*Physeter catodon, Sperm Whale
Kogia breviceps, Pygmy Sperm Whale: Atlantic and Pacific coasts
K. simus, Dwarf Sperm Whale: Atlantic and Pacific coasts

Family Monodontidae
Monodontids

*Delphinapterus leucas, White Whale or Beluga
*Monodon monoceros, Narwhal

Family Delphinidae
Delphinids

Stenella dubia, Spotted Porpoise: Atlantic and Pacific coasts
*S. longirostris, Spinner Dolphin
S. coeruleoalba, Striped Porpoise: Atlantic and Pacific coasts
Steno bredanensis, Rough-toothed Porpoise: Atlantic and Pacific coasts
*Delphinus delphis, Common or Saddle-backed Dolphin
*Tursiops truncatus, Bottlenose Dolphin
T. gillii, Gill's Bottlenose Dolphin: Pacific coast
Lissodelphis borealis, Northern Right-whale Dolphin: Pacific coast
Lagenorhynchus albirostris, White-beaked Dolphin: Atlantic coast
L. acutus, Atlantic White-sided Dolphin: Atlantic coast
L. obliquidens, Pacific White-sided Dolphin: Pacific coast
*Orcinus orca, Killer Whale
Grampus griseus, Grampus or Risso's Dolphin: Atlantic and Pacific coasts
Pseudorca crassidens, False Killer Whale: Atlantic and Pacific coasts
*Globicephala melaena, Long-finned Pilot Whale
*G. macrorhynchus, Short-finned Pilot Whale
Feresa attenuatus, Pygmy Killer Whale: Gulf coast
*Phocoena phocoena, Harbor Porpoise
*Phocoenoides dalli, Dall's Porpoise

Family Eschrichtiidae
Gray Whale

*Eschrichtius robustus, Gray Whale

Family Balaenopteridae
Balaenopterid Whales

*Balaenoptera physalus, Fin Whale
*B. borealis, Sei Whale or Rorqual
*B. acutorostrata, Little Piked or Minke Whale
*B. edeni, Bryde's Whale
*B. musculus, Blue or Sulphur-bottomed Whale
*Megaptera novaeangliae, Humpback Whale

Family Balaenidae
Right and Bowhead Whales

*Balaena glacialis, Right Whale
*B. mysticetus, Bowhead or Arctic Right Whale

Order Carnivora Carnivores

Family Canidae
Canids

*Canis latrans, Coyote
*C. rufus, Red Wolf
*C. lupus, Gray Wolf

*Alopex lagopus, Arctic Fox
*Vulpes vulpes, Red Fox
*V. macrotis, Kit Fox
*V. velox, Swift Fox
*Urocyon cinereoargenteus, Gray Fox
U. littoralis, Insular Gray Fox: islands off SW Calif.

Family Ursidae
Bears

*Ursus americanus, Black Bear
*U. arctos, Grizzly or Alaskan Brown Bear
*U. maritimus, Polar Bear

Family Procyonidae
Procyonids

*Bassariscus astutus, Ringtail
*Procyon lotor, Raccoon
*Nasua nasua, Coati

Family Mustelidae
Mustelids

*Martes americana, Marten
*M. pennanti, Fisher
*Mustela erminea, Ermine
*M. nivalis, Least Weasel
*M. frenata, Long-tailed Weasel
*M. nigripes, Black-footed Ferret
*M. vison, Mink
M. macrodon, Sea Mink [EXTINCT]
*Gulo gulo, Wolverine
*Taxidea taxus, Badger
*Spilogale putorius, Spotted Skunk
*Mephitis mephitis, Striped Skunk
*M. macroura, Hooded Skunk
*Conepatus mesoleucus, Hog-nosed Skunk
*C. leuconotus, Eastern Hog-nosed Skunk: S Tex., E Mex.
*Lutra canadensis, River Otter
*Enhydra lutris, Sea Otter

Family Felidae
Cats

*Panthera onca, Jaguar
*Felis concolor, Mountain Lion
*F. pardalis, Ocelot
*F. wiedii, Margay
*F. yagouaroundi, Jaguarundi
*F. lynx, Lynx
*F. rufus, Bobcat

Order Pinnipedia Pinnipeds

Family Otariidae
Eared Seals

*Callorhinus ursinus, Northern Fur Seal
*Arctocephalus townsendi, Guadalupe Fur Seal
*Eumetopias jubata, Northern Sea Lion
*Zalophus californianus, California Sea Lion

Family Odobenidae
Walrus

*Odobenus rosmarus, Walrus

Family Phocidae
Hair Seals

*Phoca vitulina, Harbor Seal
*P. fasciata, Ribbon Seal
*P. hispida, Ringed Seal
*Pagophilus groenlandicus, Harp Seal
Erignathus barbatus, Bearded Seal: Bering Sea, Hudson Bay, Ungava Bay
*Halichoerus grypus, Gray Seal
Monachus tropicalis, West Indian Seal: Fla., West Indies, Cen. Amer.
*Cystophora cristata, Hooded Seal
*Mirounga angustirostris, Northern Elephant Seal

Order Sirenia Sea Cows

Family Trichechidae
Manatees

*Trichechus manatus, Manatee

Order Artiodactyla
Even-toed Ungulates

Family Tayassuidae
Peccaries

*Dicotyles tajacu, Collared Peccary

Family Cervidae
Cervids

*Cervus elaphus, Elk or Wapiti
*Odocoileus hemionus, Mule Deer
*O. virginianus, White-tailed Deer
*Alces alces, Moose
*Rangifer tarandus, Caribou

Family Antilocapridae
Pronghorn

*Antilocapra americana, Pronghorn

Family Bovidae
Bovids

*Bison bison, Bison
*Oreamnos americanus, Mountain Goat
*Ovibos moschatus, Muskox
*Ovis canadensis, Bighorn Sheep
*O. dalli, Dall's Sheep

Authors & Reference Notes

Animals for All Seasons
Ronald M. Nowak, consultant for this book, serves as staff specialist with the U. S. Fish and Wildlife Service's Office of Endangered Species. Author of some 30 papers and articles of scientific and popular interest, Dr. Nowak currently is co-editing the fourth edition of Ernest P. Walker's *Mammals of the World,* scheduled for publication in 1981. For additional reading, Dr. Nowak suggests *The Mammals of North America* by E. Raymond Hall and Keith R. Kelson; *The Mammals of Canada* by A.W.F. Banfield; *The Wild Mammals of Missouri* by Charles W. Schwartz and Elizabeth R. Schwartz; and *Mammalogy* by Harvey L. Gunderson.

The Opossum
Alfred L. Gardner, a research biologist with the National Fish and Wildlife Laboratory, Washington, D. C., is an associate editor of the *Journal of Mammalogy* and the author of numerous articles dealing with mammalian systematics, biogeography, and evolution. Suggested reading: *The Biology of Marsupials,* edited by B. Stonehouse and D. Gilmore; *Life of Marsupials* by Hugh Tyndale-Biscoe; and *Possums* by Carl G. Hartman.

Shrews & Moles
John L. Paradiso is a senior staff biologist with the U. S. Fish and Wildlife Service's Office of Endangered Species. He was the editor of the third edition (1975) of Walker's *Mammals of the World* and, with Dr. Nowak, is co-editor of the forthcoming fourth edition. He is the author of a "Checklist of the Mammals of Assateague Island," *Mammals of Maryland,* and a number of status reports on North American mammals. Suggested reading: *Mammals of Wisconsin* by Hartley H. T. Jackson.

Bats
Merlin D. Tuttle, curator of mammals at the Milwaukee Public Museum, is also an adjunct associate professor at Marquette University and the University of Wisconsin-Milwaukee. He is the author of many papers on bats and is best known for his studies of the ecology and behavior of gray bats in the southeastern United States. Suggested reading: *Bats of America* by Roger W. Barbour and Wayne H. Davis; *Listening in the Dark* by Donald R. Griffin; *The World of Bats* by Nina Leen and Alvin Novick; *The Lives of Bats* by D. W. Yalden and P. A. Morris.

The Armadillo
Ralph M. Wetzel, professor of biology at the University of Connecticut, is the author or co-author of numerous articles in scientific journals. His interest in Edentata and neotropical carnivores has led to extensive field work in North and South America. Suggested reading: "Zoogeography of the Nine-Banded Armadillo" by Stephen R. Humphrey, in *BioScience,* August 1974; *The Armadillo* by Roy V. Talmadge and G. Dale Buchanan, Rice Institute Monograph in Biology, Vol. 41, No. 2, 1954.

Rabbits, Hares & Pikas
Joseph A. Chapman is a professor of ecology and wildlife science and head of the University of Maryland's Appalachian Environmental Laboratory in Frostburg. He is the author or co-author of numerous technical papers and articles and co-editor of the forthcoming volume, *Game, Pest, and Commercial Mammals of North America.* Suggested reading: *The Private Life of the Rabbit* by R. M. Lockley, *The Little-Known Pika* by Robert T. Orr.

Gnawing Mammals
Hugh H. Genoways, curator of mammals for the Carnegie Museum of Natural History, Pittsburgh, is a director of the American Society of Mammalogists and former managing editor of the *Journal of Mammalogy.* With special interest in New World bats and rodents, he is the author or co-author of more than 80 technical papers and articles. Suggested reading: *Rodents, Their Lives and Habits* by Peter W. Hanney and *Squirrels of North America* by Dorcas MacClintock.

Whales Great & Small
Victor B. Scheffer was for 30 years a research biologist for the U. S. government, specializing in marine mammals. He served as a member of the State Department's first team of Antarctic Observers. His work has earned such awards as the John Burroughs Medal, the Joseph Wood Krutch Award, and the Department of the Interior's Distinguished Service Award. Now retired, Dr. Scheffer serves as consultant to the U. S. Marine Mammal Commission. His many books include *The Year of the Whale, A Voice for Wildlife,* and *A Natural History of Marine Mammals.* Suggested further reading: *Whales and Dolphins* by Everhard J. Slijper and *Mind in the Waters: A Book to Celebrate the Consciousness of Whales and Dolphins,* edited by Joan McIntyre.

Meat Eaters
Maurice G. Hornocker, leader of the Idaho Cooperative Wildlife Research Unit, is currently conducting studies in predator ecology and management of the badger, wolverine, river otter, and leopard. His research on big cats has taken him to four continents and led to many technical and popular articles as well as film documentaries. Dr. Hornocker is a member of the Advisory Committee on the Felidae of

the International Union for Conservation of Nature (IUCN). Suggested reading: *The Carnivores* by R. F. Ewer.

Charles Jonkel is a professor of research and wildlife biology at the University of Montana and an editor of *Canadian Field Naturalist.* He has helped organize several bear conservation and study groups, including the IUCN Polar Bear Specialists Group. He serves as president of the International Bear Biology Association. Suggested reading: *Grizzly Country* by Andy Russell; *Big Game of North America: Ecology and Management,* edited by J. L. Schmidt and D. L. Gilbert; and *Proceedings of the 1975 Predator Symposium,* edited by Robert L. Phillips and Charles Jonkel.

L. David Mech is a wildlife research biologist with the U. S. Fish and Wildlife Service and adjunct professor with the Department of Ecology and Behavioral Biology, University of Minnesota. His interest in wolves and other carnivores has taken him from Africa to India, from Italy to the U.S.S.R. A prolific writer, he is the author of some 150 articles and books. Suggested reading: *Coyotes: Biology, Behavior, and Management,* edited by Marc Bekoff, and *The Wolf* by L. David Mech.

Seals, Sea Lions & Walruses

Karl W. Kenyon has retired after more than 25 years as a wildlife research biologist with the U. S. Fish and Wildlife Service, but he continues to participate in government studies of monk seals and sea otters. He is also a member of the Committee of Scientific Advisors to the U. S. Marine Mammal Commission and the author of more than 100 articles and reports, chiefly on oceanic birds and mammals. Suggested reading: *Marine Mammals,* edited by Delphine Haley; *Seals, Sea Lions, and Walruses* by Victor B. Scheffer.

The Manatee

Howard W. Campbell, a zoologist with the National Fish and Wildlife Laboratory in Gainesville, Florida, currently serves as leader of the Southeast Ecology Project. He is also chairman of the IUCN Crocodile Specialists Group and has published widely on subjects ranging from bog turtles in Maryland to poisonous snakes in Southeast Asia. Suggested reading: *Biological Synopsis of the Manatee* by K. Ronald, L. J. Selley, and E. C. Amoroso; and *Hunted Mammals of the Sea* by Robert M. McClung.

Hoofed Mammals

Valerius Geist is associate dean and professor of environmental science at the University of Calgary. In addition he serves on several national and international ecological commissions, including the Canadian Government's Arctic Land Use Committee. His books include *Mountain Sheep: A Study in Behavior and Evolution; Mountain Sheep and Man in the Northern Wilds;* and *Life Strategies, Human Adaptations, Environmental Design.* Suggested reading: *The Behaviour of Ungulates,* edited by V. Geist and F. Walther; *The North American Buffalo* by Frank G. Roe; and *North American Moose* by Randolph L. Peterson.

Alien Mammals

Stephen R. Seater has written extensively on various aspects of wildlife conservation. While serving as Staff Biologist for the World Wildlife Fund, he helped to launch Operation Tiger, designed to save India's vanishing tiger population. He also served as executive director of the Urban Wildlife Research Center. Suggested reading: *America's Last Wild Horses* by Hope Ryden; *Animal Movers* by George Laycock; and *Animal Invaders* by Clive Roots.

The Ultimate Mammal

Dr. Nowak, also author of the closing chapter, suggests the following books for additional reading: *Extinct and Vanishing Mammals of the Western Hemisphere* by Glover M. Allen; *Wildlife in America* by Peter Matthiessen; and *Vanishing Wildlife of North America* by Thomas B. Allen.

In addition to the works cited above, the editors found the following regional guides especially valuable and interesting: *A Field Guide to the Mammals* by William H. Burt and Richard P. Grossenheider (The Peterson Field Guide Series); *Wild Mammals of New England* by Alfred J. Godin; *The Mammals of Louisiana and Its Adjacent Waters* by George H. Lowery, Jr.; *Mammals of the Pacific States* by Lloyd G. Ingles; and *Wildlife of Mexico* by A. Starker Leopold. Classics in the field of animal studies include *The Quadrupeds of North America* (3 volumes, 1854) by John James Audubon and John Bachman, and *Lives of Game Animals* (4 volumes, 1928) by Ernest Thompson Seton.

Acknowledgments

The editors are indebted to many wildlife researchers throughout the Nearctic Realm for their assistance with this book. In particular we wish to thank Dr. Fred H. Harrington of Mount Saint Vincent University, Halifax, and Dr. Howard McCarley of Austin College, Sherman, Texas, for providing the taped canid howls, and David M. Seager, for annotating the howls. We are also grateful for the assistance provided by staff members of the Smithsonian Institution, and especially Dr. Charles O. Handley, Jr., Curator of Mammals. Generous aid was given by Dr. E. Raymond Hall of the University of Kansas Museum of Natural History; Dr. Donald R. Griffin of The Rockefeller University; Dr. Don E. Wilson, Chief, Mammal Section, National Fish and Wildlife Laboratory; Michael J. Smolen of the Carnegie Museum of Natural History; Dr. Charles Dauphine of the Canadian Wildlife Service; Dr. Curtis J. Carley of the U. S. Fish and Wildlife Service Red Wolf Relocation Project; staff members of the Arizona-Sonora Desert Museum, Tucson, Arizona; Dr. Eleanor Storrs, Medical Research Institute, Florida Institute of Technology; staff members of the National Park Service; Dr. James A. Lackey of the American Society of Mammalogists; Aubrey Watson, Tennessee Wildlife Resources Agency; Lowell Georgia; Dr. Robert C. Farentinos; David R. Klein, Alaska Cooperative Wildlife Research Unit; and Dr. Charles Meslow, Oregon Cooperative Wildlife Research Unit.

The prairie dog burrow illustration on page 120 was re-drawn, by permission, from "Organisms That Capture Currents" by Steven Vogel, © 1978 by Scientific American, Inc.

Illustration Credits

139, Jim Brandenburg. 140 (top), Jim Brandenburg. (bottom), Wolfgang Bayer. 141 (top), Robert Hynes. (bottom), Jen and Des Bartlett. 142, Jim Brandenburg. 143, William J. Weber. 144 (left), Alvin E. Staffan, Photo Researchers. (right), Roger W. Barbour. 145 (top), John Ebeling. (bottom), Jeff Foott. 146-147, James A. Sullivan. 148 (left), William J. Weber. (right), Roger W. Barbour. 149, Alvin E. Staffan, Photo Researchers. 150, William E. Grenfell, Jr. 151 (left), William J. Weber. (right), Alvin E. Staffan. 152 (top), George Olin. (bottom), Robert Hynes. 153 (left), Gary R. Jones, Bruce Coleman Inc. (right), Edgar T. Jones. 154 (left), Michael Wotton. (right), Alvin E. Staffan. 155, Alvin E. Staffan. 156 (left), Karl H. Maslowski. (right), G. C. Kelley. 157, Jim Brandenburg. 158-159, Jim Brandenburg. 160 (top), David Gill, National Museums of Canada. (bottom), Robert Hynes. 161 (left), James W. Helmericks. (right), Roger W. Barbour. 162, Alvin E. Staffan. 163 (top), Tom Brakefield, Bruce Coleman Inc. (bottom), Robert Hynes. 164-165, John Ebeling. 165, Gary R. Zahm.

Whales Great & Small
166, Entheos. 168-169, Al Giddings, Sea Films, Inc. 170-171, Robert Vile, Sea World, Inc. 171, Robert French, Sea World, Inc. 173, Bates Littlehales, National Geographic Photographer. 175, Bill Curtsinger. 176-177, Al Giddings, Sea Films, Inc. 178-205, paintings by Richard Ellis. 202-203, courtesy of Richard J. Wehle. 206-207, Thomas Nebbia.

Meat Eaters
208, Maurice G. Hornocker. 210, Robert Hynes. 212, Sabra K. McCracken. 212-213, Rolf O. Peterson. 214, Erwin A. Bauer. 216-

217, Rollie Ostermick. 219, Jim Brandenburg. 220, Harry Engels. 221, Jonathan T. Wright, Bruce Coleman Inc. 222, Robert Hynes. 223, Ralph H. Williams. 224, Tom W. Hall. 225, Jim Brandenburg. 226 (left), Tom McHugh. (right), James W. Helmericks. 227, Lynn L. Rogers. 228-229, Lynn L. Rogers. 230 (left), Rod Allin, Bruce Coleman Inc. (right), Glenn D. Chambers. 231, Steve Maslowski. 233, Angelo Lomeo. 234, Tom McHugh, Wildlife Unlimited. 235, Lynn L. Rogers. 236-237, Stewart Cassidy. 237, Steven C. Kaufman. 238-239, W. Randy Brandon, Third Eye Photography. 240-241, W. Randy Brandon, Third Eye Photography. 242-243, Douglas H. Chadwick. 243 (top), R. E. Schweinsburg, N.W.T. Wildlife Service. (bottom), Robert Hynes. 244-245, Alan S. Fetting. 246, Lois and George Cox. 247, Entheos. 248, Bates Littlehales, National Geographic Photographer. 249, Vince Cavaleri. 250-251, Vince Cavaleri. 253, Jeff Foott. 254, Ed Cesar, National Film Board Phototheque. 255, Roger A. Powell. 256 (top), Tom McHugh, Photo Researchers. (bottom), Diane Ensign-Caughey. 257 (left), Bob and Clara Calhoun, Bruce Coleman Inc. (right), Alvin E. Staffan. 258 (left), Luther C. Goldman. (right), Karl H. Maslowski. 259, Stewart Cassidy. 260, Alvin E. Staffan. 261, Lois and George Cox. 262, George Olin. 263 (left), Jim Anderson. (right), William J. Weber. (bottom), Robert Hynes. 264, John M. Burnley, Bruce Coleman Inc. 265 (top), Bill Browning. (bottom), Ed Park. 266, Robert F. Sisson, National Geographic Photographer. 267 (left), Bates Littlehales, Na-

tional Geographic Photographer. (top right), Jeff Foott. (bottom right), Jeff Foott, Bruce Coleman Inc. 268, Robert Hynes. 269, Hälle Flygare. 270, Maurice G. Hornocker. 271, Leonard Lee Rue III. 272-273, Maurice G. Hornocker. 274, E. R. Degginger. 275, Warren Garst, Tom Stack & Associates. 276, Raymond A. Mendez, Animals Animals. 277, Tom McHugh. 278, Tom W. Hall. 279, Leonard Lee Rue III. 280, Clyde H. Smith. 281, Jerry T. Smith.

Seals, Sea Lions & Walruses
282, Tom Walker. 284, Jeff Foott. 285, Jeremiah S. Sullivan, The Photo Circle. 286, Jonathan Blair. 288-289, Entheos. 290-291, Fred Bruemmer. 292, E. R. Degginger. 293, Entheos. 294, Jeff Foott, Bruce Coleman Inc. 294-295, Jen and Des Bartlett. 296-297, Leonard Lee Rue III, Tom Stack & Associates. 298 (top), Fred Bruemmer. (bottom), Brian Milne. 299, Tom Walker. 300-301, Tupper Ansel Blake. 302 (left), Larry M. Shults. (top right), Carleton Ray, Photo Researchers. (bottom), Robert Hynes. 303, Fred Bruemmer. 304-305, Fred Bruemmer. 306, David Cavagnaro. 307, Robert B. Evans.

The Manatee
308, James A. Powell. 310-311, James A. Sugar. 311, Jeff Foott.

Hoofed Mammals
312, Jim Brandenburg. 314, Stephen J. Krasemann. 315, William J. Weber. 316-317, R. Steven Fuller. 318, Tom W. Hall. 319, Douglas H. Chadwick. 321, Wilbur M. Mills. 322, Stephen J. Krasemann. 323, Joe Branney, Tom Stack & Associates. 324-325, W. E. Ruth. 326-327, R. Steven Fuller. 328, Bill Browning. 329, Diane Ensign-Caughey. 330-331, Stewart Cassidy. 331, Marty Stouffer Productions, Animals Animals. 332-333, Jerry T. Smith. 334-335, Jim Brandenburg. 336, W. E. Ruth.

337, Wayne Towriss. 338-339, Jim Brandenburg. 340, Stephen J. Krasemann. 341, Douglas H. Chadwick. 342, Arthur T. Bergerud. 343, S. D. MacDonald, National Museums of Canada. 344, Robert Hynes. 344-345, David W. Kitchen. 346-347, Michael S. Sample. 348-349, William Albert Allard. 350, Rick McIntyre. 351, Tom W. Hall. 352-353, Tom McHugh. 354-355, Douglas H. Chadwick. 356-357, Fred Bruemmer. 358-359, Stephen J. Krasemann. 359, Wayne Towriss. 360-361, Larry Aiuppy. 361, Stewart Cassidy. 362-363, Galen A. Rowell. 363, Jim Whitcomb. 364-365, John S. Crawford.

Alien Mammals
366, David Doubilet. 368-369, Ed Dutch. 370-371, Ed Dutch. 373, Franz J. Camenzind. 374-375, Jonathan T. Wright, Bruce Coleman Inc. 376 (left), J. Markham, Bruce Coleman Inc. (right), John R. MacGregor, Peter Arnold, Inc. 377, Tom McHugh. 378, Thase Daniel. 379, Hans Reinhard, Bruce Coleman Inc. 380, Jim Whitcomb, Texas Parks & Wildlife. 381, Patricia Moehlman.

The Ultimate Mammal
382, Al Giddings, Sea Films, Inc. 385, Dick Randall. 386-387, Emory Kristof, National Geographic Photographer. 388, Jim Brandenburg. 390-391, Jim Brandenburg. 392-393, R. Steven Fuller.

Index

Illustrations are indicated in **boldface;** illustrated biographies in **boldface** with asterisk (*); picture captions in *italic;* text references in light type.

Type composition by National Geographic's Photographic Services. Color separations by Beck Engraving Co., Inc., Philadelphia, Pa.; Chanticleer Company, Inc., New York, N.Y.; Graphic Color Plate, Inc., Stamford, Conn.; Lanman Companies, Washington, D. C.; J. Wm. Reed Company, Alexandria, Va. Paper by Mead Corp., Publishing Paper Division, New York, N.Y.; S. D. Warren Company, Bladensburg, Md.; Westvaco Corp., New York, N.Y.; P. H. Glatfelter Company, Spring Grove, Pa. Printing and binding by Kingsport Press, Kingsport, Tenn.

Library of Congress CIP Data
Main entry under title:
Wild Animals of North America
(Natural Science Library)
    Includes index.
    1. Mammals—North America.
I. National Geographic Society, Washington, D. C.
QL715.W54   599'.097   79-18452
ISBN 0-87044-294-5